Geography 2000

Landscapes and People

Brian Greasley

Adviser for Humanities
Sheffield L.E.A.

and

Martin Shevill

Head of Geography and Geology
King Edward VII School
Sheffield

Nelson

Thomas Nelson and Sons Ltd
Nelson House Mayfield Road
Walton-on-Thames Surrey
KT12 5PL UK

51 York Place
Edinburgh
EH1 3JD UK

Thomas Nelson (Hong Kong) Ltd
Toppan Building 10/F
22A Westlands Road
Quarry Bay Hong Kong

Thomas Nelson Australia
102 Dodds Street
South Melbourne
Victoria 3205 Australia

Nelson Canada
1120 Birchmount Road
Scarborough Ontario
M1K 5G4 Canada

© Brian Greasley and Martin Shevill 1989

First published by Macmillan Education Ltd 1989
(under ISBN 0-333-43786-1)

This edition published by Thomas Nelson and Sons Ltd 1992

ISBN 0-17-438567-6

NPN 9 8 7 6 5 4 3

All rights reserved. No paragraph of this publication may be reproduced, copied or transmitted save with written permission or in accordance with the provisions of the Copyright, Design and Patents Act 1988, or under the terms of any licence permitting limited copying issued by the Copyright Licensing Agency, 90 Tottenham Court Road, London W1P 9HE.

Any person who does any unauthorised act in relation to this publication may be liable to criminal prosecution and civil claims for damages.

Printed in Hong Kong.

Acknowledgements

The authors and publishers wish to acknowledge the following photograph sources:

Anglian Water pp 50, 61; Barnaby's Picture Library pp 34, 66, 68; Jim Brownbill p 28; Camera Press p 56; J Allen Cash Ltd pp 21, 59, 80; Bruce Coleman p 63; G.S.F. Picture Library pp 44, 52, 55, 56, 79, 83; National Meteorological Library p 39; National Trust Photographic Library p 43; Science Photo Library p 70; Sheffield City Council/Planning Dept p 18; Bob Weller p 80, 81.
Cover photograph Robert Harding Picture Library.
The remaining photographs were taken by the authors.

The publishers have made every effort to trace the copyright holders, but where they have failed to do so they will be pleased to make the necessary arrangements at the first opportunity.

Illustrations by Lynn Williams and Ursula Sieger

Contents

Preface 4

1 An Enquiry
Where to site a garden? 6

2 Valleys
The Shirebrook 18

3 Floods
A natural hazard 26

4 Weather
Rain or shine? 34

5 Coasts
Why coasts change 42

6 Volcanoes
The power of the earth 52

7 Lowlands
Changing environments 60

8 Uplands
Using the uplands 68

9 Landscapes
Two contrasting areas 78

Preface

Geography 2000 Note to the Teacher

This series of four books provides the required learning in Geography for pupils at Key Stage 3. Although the texts could be used in sequence, they are flexible enough for either a course to be designed using elements from each, or for sections to be used within existing courses.

The series covers Attainment Targets 2, 3 and 4 with the integration of Attainment Targets 1 and 5: Geographical Skills and Environmental Issues in all four tests.

Landscapes and People covers the key elements of AT3 Physical geography.

Environments and People covers key elements of AT2 with examples taken from the UK, Europe and the wider world. AT4, Human Geography is examined at UK and European scales and AT3 Physical Geography looks at major world ecosystems.

People and Planning covers key areas of AT4, Human Geography, with examples taken from the UK, thus giving a comprehensive coverage of themes and regions to assist with teaching of AT2.

People and World Issues covers key elements of AT2 with regard to the wider world and AT4, Human Geography.

The Approach throughout is designed to present the pupil with a sense of challenge and purpose, through the focus in each section on a relevant question or issue, and through the tasks it is suggested pupils undertake. The scheme encourages pupil involvement at all stages by developing an investigative approach and providing opportunity for individual, pair and group work. Each pupil is encouraged to acquire knowledge relevant to the investigation, comprehend material presented, develop informed opinions and reach conclusions in relation to a particular question or issue.

The Learning Experiences have been developed to allow pupils to approach questions and issues from a variety of viewpoints and perspectives. The pupil is fully involved in the process of investigation at all stages, and it is anticipated that there will be opportunity for parallel or further investigation using the techniques in the local area. Within the texts, data is provided in a variety of forms such as maps, statistics, graphs, photographs, pictures, and in written form as newspaper extracts, text and letters.

The Format follows a common pattern throughout, with each investigation being introduced with a clear statement of aims. Background information is presented in a variety of forms; blocks of text have been reduced to a minimum, and information sections introduced where appropriate. Required terminology is defined in the context where it is first introduced. The tasks are carefully structured to allow for a full understanding and to ensure that pupils with a range of ability may reach satisfactory conclusions and reach their own potential.

Progression is achieved by moving from small to larger scale investigations and from the familiar to the unfamiliar. More sophisticated data and techniques are introduced to provide the information required to reach conclusions; this is particularly so in **People and Planning** and **People and World Issues** which build on learning developed in **Landscapes and People** and **Environments and People**. Ideas and concepts and a framework of skills and techniques are developed progressively through the series.

Chapter/Context
1 An Enquiry Where to site a garden?
2 Valleys The Shirebrook
3 Floods A natural hazard
4 Weather Rain or shine?
5 Coasts Why coasts change
6 Volcanoes The power of the earth
7 Lowland Changing environments
8 Uplands Using the uplands
9 Landscapes Two contrasting areas

Landscapes and People

This text illustrates the interrelationships between people and the changing features of the landscape by focusing on a series of issues and questions. The processes of physical geography are outlined within a context which requires each pupil to use the knowledge gained through the application of suitable skills and techniques, some of which are common to each chapter, such as decision making and the analysis of a range of information to reach appropriate conclusions. The text comprehensively covers the Programmes of Study at Key Stage 3.

Examples of Themes/Ideas from Programmes of Study	Examples of National Curriculum Attainment Targets	Skills	Values/Attitudes
• How site conditions can influence temperature, wind speed. • To investigate and compare the colour, texture and organic content of different types of soil. • To enquire into geographical processes both inside and outside the classroom. To see how natural and human made conditions influence people's decisions. • To make accurate measurements of geographical features and conditions.	1.4, 1.7, 1.6, 3.4	—Analysis of plan and photograph —Measurement of infiltration —Analysis of soil – texture, depth and acidity —Measurement of slope – use of clinometer —Use of compass —Measurement of wind direction and strength —Measurement of temperature —Draw a bar graph	—Consideration of the delicate interrelationships within the environment
• To identify and describe landscape features. eg. hills, valleys. • To study landforms related to river channels and valleys. • The main features of river basins. • The processes which form the features associated with river channels and river valleys. • The factors that influence stream flow in a river basin.	1.3, 1.4, 1.5, 1.6, 3.3, 3.4, 3.6, 3.7	—Analysis of air photographs and maps —Understanding of cross-section —Labelling diagrams —Use of visual interest table —Survey work of measuring the flow of a river and the cross-section of a river	—The need for reclamation of derelict landscapes —The importance of preserving aspects of the landscape of particular interest
• The causes and effects of river floods and methods used to reduce flood risk. • The main components and links in the hydrological cycle. • The processes which form the features associated with river valleys.	1.6, 3.3, 3.4, 3.5, 3.6, 3.7, 5.6	—Analysis of maps – Atlas work —Ability to draw bar graphs —Analysis of photographs —Use of climate graph —Measurement of area on a map	—That some people live under constant threat of the natural environment —Managing the environment has an economic cost
• The difference between weather and climate. • The effects of relief, convection and fronts on rainfall. • Seasonal patterns of temperature and rainfall over the British Isles. • To compare the main characteristics and distribution patterns of the British climate and how it is influenced by latitude. • How weather in the British Isles is influenced by anticyclones and depressions.	1.3, 1.7, 3.5, 3.6, 3.7	—Analysis and construction of climate graph —The use of weather instruments —Analysis of weather maps —Comparison of data on maps —Recording weather information	
• The landforms associated with coasts. eg. cliffs, wave cut platforms, stacks, beaches and spits. • The processes which form features associated with coasts.	3.3, 3.6, 3.7	—Analysis of maps —Relating photographs to maps —Survey techniques for longshore drift —Analysis of collected data —Measurement of slope – use of clinometer —Drawing line graph	—That conflicting interests need to be resolved to provide solutions to issues
• Physical processes which can give rise to one type of natural hazard and how people respond to that hazard. • The nature and effects of volcanic eruptions and the production of craters, cones and lava flows. To investigate the global distribution of earthquakes and volcanoes and how these relate to the boundaries of crustal plates.	1.5, 1.6, 3.4. 3.5, 3.6	—Atlas work —Analysing maps —Sketching —Annotating —Creative writing —Group work	—That people live under constant threat of the natural environment —Managing the natural environment has economic and careful management implications
• Ecological food chains. • The ways in which people look after environments and to consider whether some environments need special protection. • How attempts to plan and manage environments have unintended effects: a case study of Norfolk's wetlands.	1.5, 3.4, 3.6	—Atlas work —Analysis of photographs —Landscape sketching and labelling —Visual interest table	—The need to conserve wildlife —An appreciation of the conflicting views of different individuals and/or groups
• To identify and describe landscape features. • The effects of frost action. • To examine different types of weathering and erosion. • How human activity can harm areas of great environmental value. • How landscapes can be modified by human action. • How areas of scenic attraction can give rise to conflicting demands on them and the issues which rise as a result. • To examine how glaciers evolve.	1.5, 1.6, 3.3, 3.5, 3.7, 4.4, 5.4, 5.6	—Analysis of photographs —Mapwork —Drawing a cross-section —Analysis of maps —Analysis of information	—That gains for some groups/individuals may be losses for others
• To identify and describe landscape features. • How geology influences drainage, soil, vegetation. • The effects of chemical and mechanical weathering and the distinction between weathering and erosion. • To investigate and compare the colour, texture and organic content of different types of soil. • How areas of scenic attraction can give rise to conflicting demands on them and the issues which rise as a result.	1.3, 1.4, 1.5, 3.3, 3.4, 3.5, 3.6, 3.7, 4.5, 5.4, 5.6, 5.7	—OS Mapwork —Analysis of photographs —Visual interest table —Analysis of rock type —Use of quadrat survey —Use of block diagram	—The need to preserve areas of outstanding beauty

Unit 1 — Where to site a garden?

AN ENQUIRY

Site B (top) and site D (bottom)

The proposal:
that a group from Carter Lodge School should make a small garden to grow flowers and vegetables somewhere in the school grounds.

Question:
where should the garden be sited?

The sites:
four possible SITES have been found, marked A, B, C, D on the map.

The task:
to decide which of the four sites would be the best one for the garden.

1 Use the map to give two differences in the LOCATION of sites B and D.

2 Use the photographs to give two other differences between sites B and D.

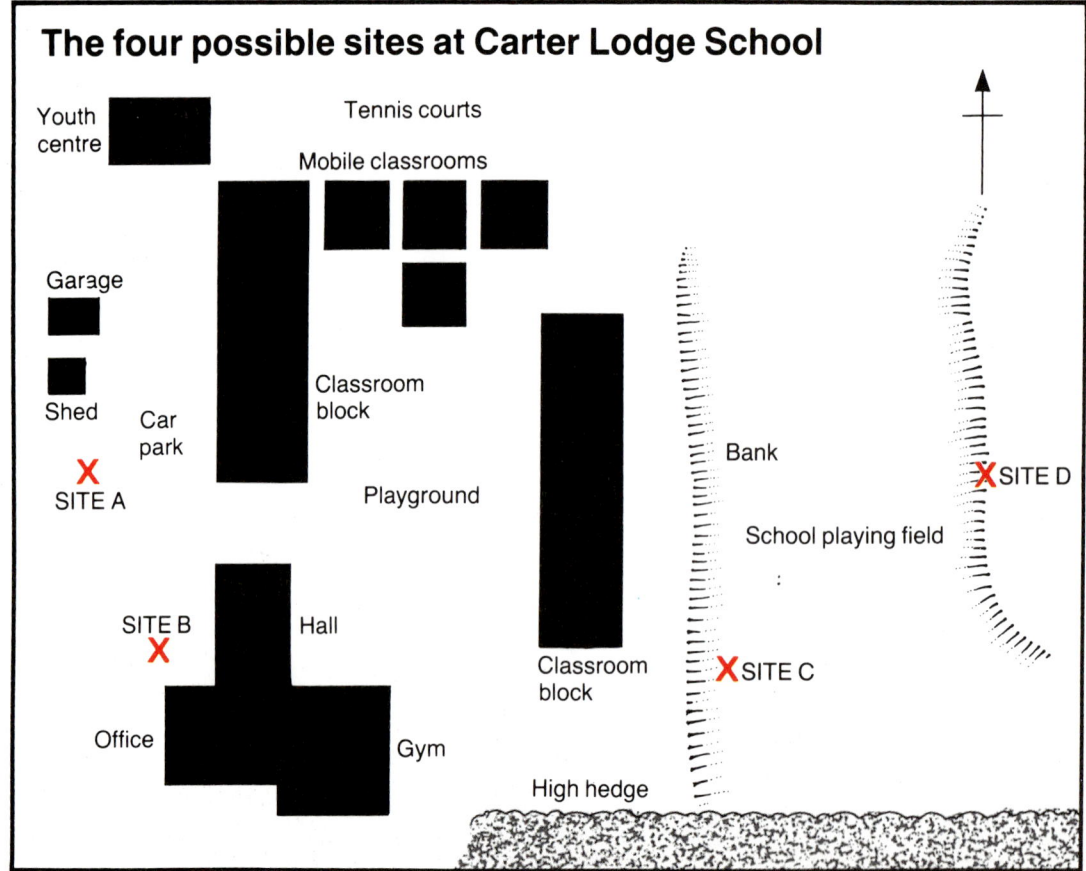

The four possible sites at Carter Lodge School

LOCATION
The exact position of a place

SITE
The piece of ground where something (the garden) is placed

What do we need to know about each site?

The best site for the garden will be the one which:

(a) is the (warmest/coolest).
(b) is (well/poorly) drained.
(c) (is/is not) sheltered from the wind.
(d) is where (many/few) people go.
(e) has the (richest/poorest) soil.
(f) is (flat/sloping) ground.

The garden is to grow plants. So we have to find out what these plants need to grow well. This tells us what we need to know about each site. Then we can choose which is the best site for a garden.

In the next few pages we will be looking carefully at each point on your chart in turn. We can then decide:
either – which site A, B, C or D is best for a garden at Carter Lodge School.
or – you could carry out the same tests at four sites around your school.

3 Copy out the chart above on 'The best site'. Choose one word from the brackets. To help you, look at the diagram below.

4 Using the information on this page write down why summer is the time of year for greatest plant growth.

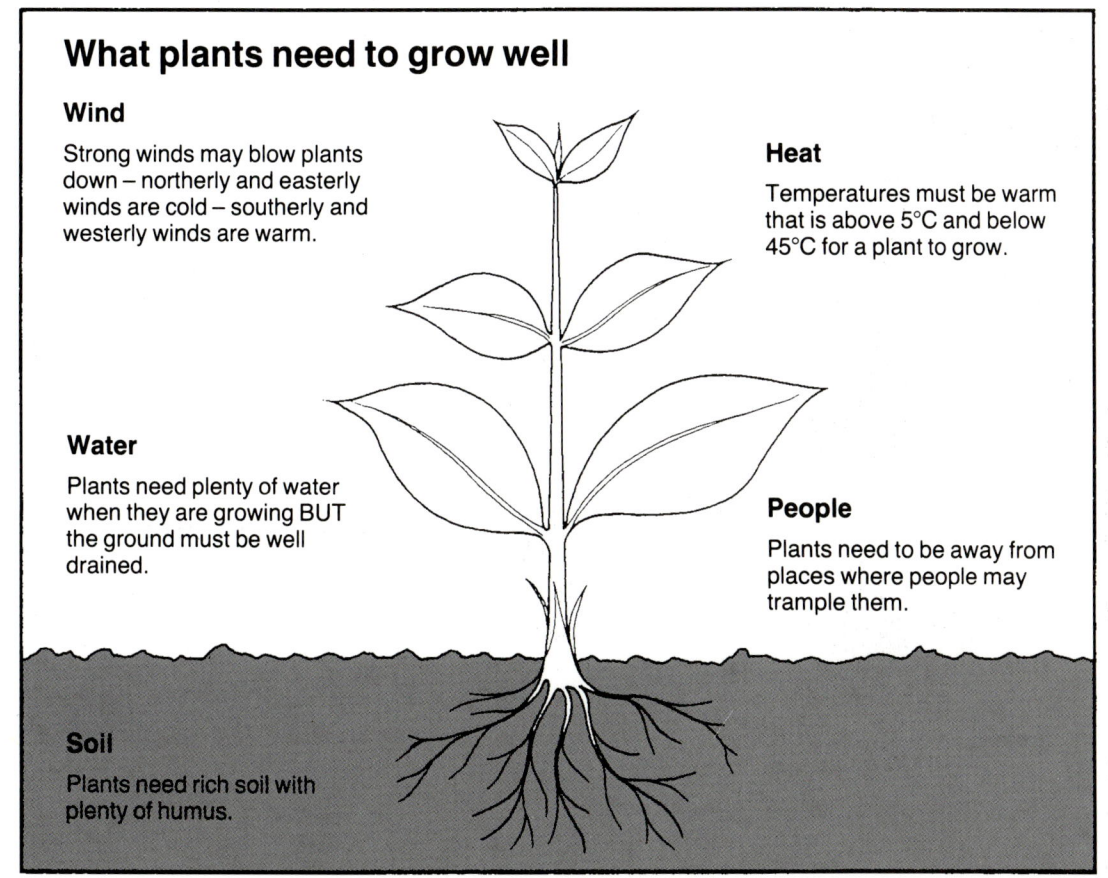

What plants need to grow well

Wind
Strong winds may blow plants down – northerly and easterly winds are cold – southerly and westerly winds are warm.

Heat
Temperatures must be warm that is above 5°C and below 45°C for a plant to grow.

Water
Plants need plenty of water when they are growing BUT the ground must be well drained.

People
Plants need to be away from places where people may trample them.

Soil
Plants need rich soil with plenty of humus.

Is the site well drained?

For the garden we need a well drained site. We need to find out which sites are well drained.
If the site is not well drained:
– the roots of the plants will be standing in water
– the plants will not grow.
If the rain-water drains straight through the soil:
– the plants will not get enough water to grow.
So we need to find a site where water drains away steadily.

We can find out if the site for the garden is well drained.

We need to measure the speed at which the water soaks into the ground. This is called INFILTRATION.

INFILTRATION
The speed at which water soaks into the ground

How do we measure infiltration?

A group of Year 8 pupils collect together the equipment needed.

– Press the plastic container into the ground until about one third of it is buried.

– Fill the measuring jar with 100cc of water. Pour the water into the ring.

– Time how long it takes all the water to soak into the ground.

– Write down the time on the recording sheet.

– Repeat the experiment three times in different places at the site.

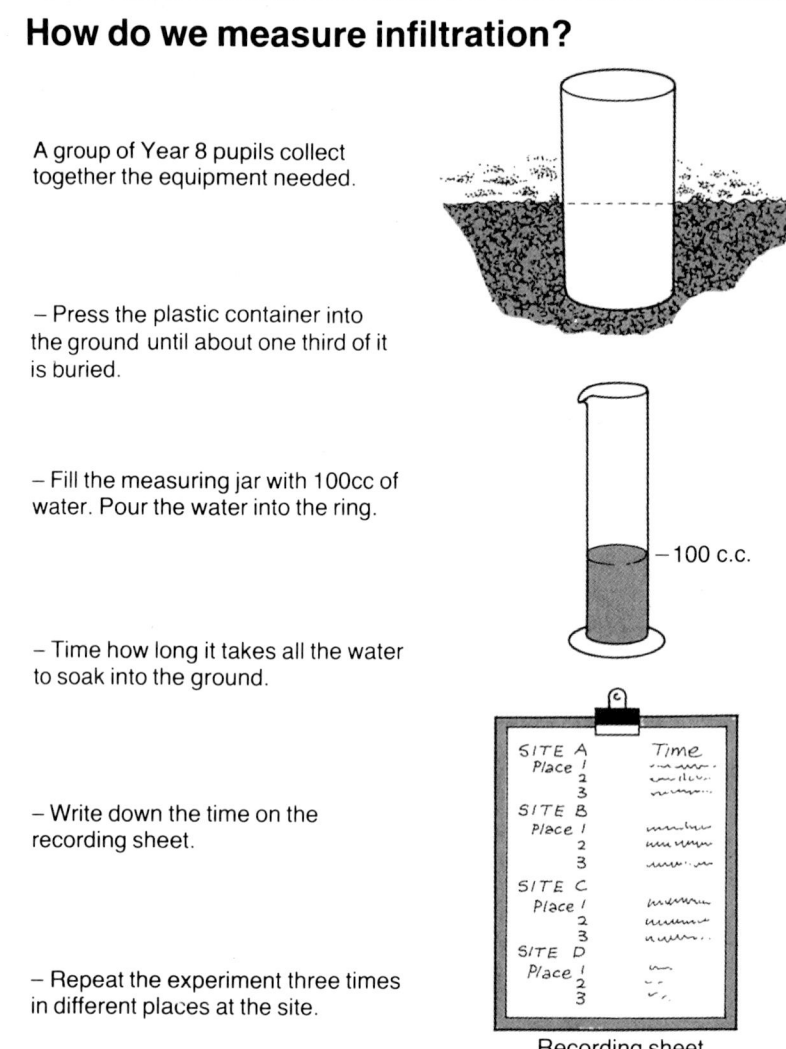

Recording sheet

What do we need to measure infiltration?

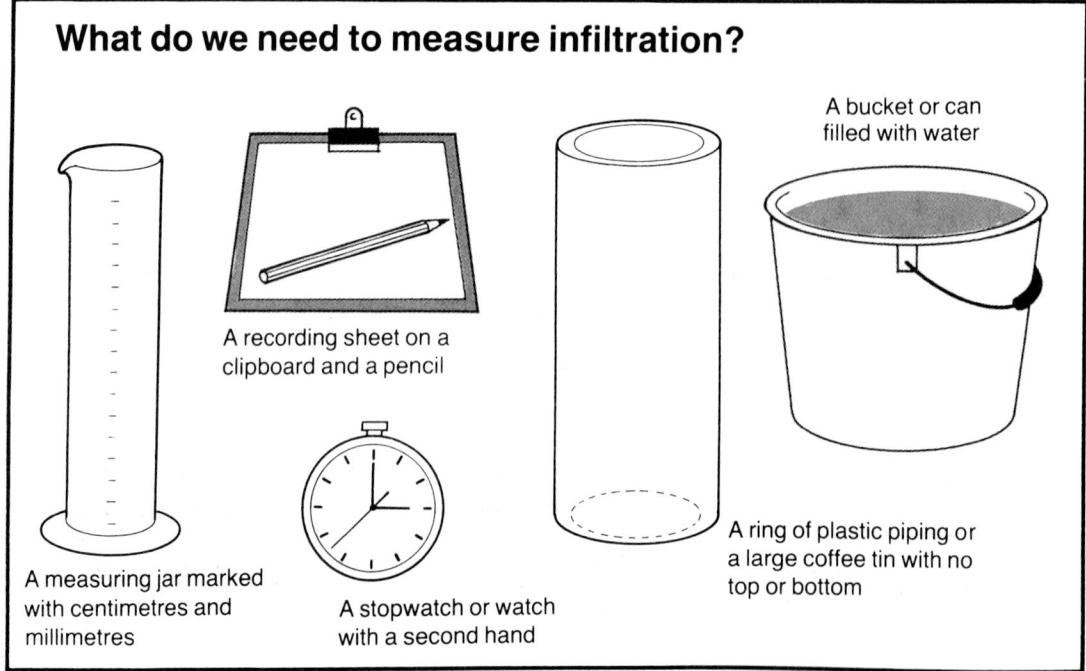

A measuring jar marked with centimetres and millimetres

A recording sheet on a clipboard and a pencil

A stopwatch or watch with a second hand

A ring of plastic piping or a large coffee tin with no top or bottom

A bucket or can filled with water

1 Why is a stopwatch needed to help to measure infiltration?

2 Look at the photograph. Write down the job being done by each person.

3 Give one reason why the slowest draining site will not be the best.

4 Give one reason why a steadily draining site will be the best.

5 Why do you need to repeat the experiment at three different places at the site?

Conducting the infiltration experiment

6 (a) Copy out the best order chart.

(b) Look at the chart of results for Carter Lodge School below.

(c) Decide which site has the best infiltration for the garden.

(d) Put the letter of the best site in 1st place.

(e) Put the other sites in order in 2nd, 3rd and 4th places.

What is the best order of sites at Carter Lodge?

Order	1st	2nd	3rd	4th
Site				

Infiltration: Results for Carter Lodge School

Site	Time taken (seconds) 1st time	2nd time	3rd time	Description of what happened at each site
Site A	58	60	59	Water soaked into the ground evenly and began as soon as it was poured in.
Site B	71	74	72	Water soaked into the ground slowly and steadily.
Site C	30	32	28	Water soaked into the ground very rapidly and began as soon as it was poured in.
Site D	149	164	156	Water soaked into the ground very slowly indeed.

Which site has the best soil?

What we need to find out about the soil

There are three important things we need to know about the soil, its depth, texture and ACIDITY.

1 Why is the best garden site where the soil has a good rich humus?

2 Look at the details of types of soil in the soil texture experiment.
(a) Choose which soil is best for the garden.
(b) Give two reasons why you think it is the best type of soil for a garden.

3 Draw a bar graph to show the level of acid in the soil for the four sites at Carter Lodge using the figures given in the 'Details of soil survey' shown opposite. (The framework of the graph is shown on point 4 of the Acidity experiment diagram.)

What is soil made of?

Water — The spaces between the particles of soil may be filled with water. The amount of water will affect the types of plants which will grow.

Air — The space between the particles may be filled with air. This allows the soil animals and the plants to breathe.

Humus — Humus is the rotted remains of plants, parts of plants and animals. This provides most of the materials which plants need to grow. A good soil will contain plenty of humus which is why gardeners often dig compost into their gardens.

Rock — The rock which makes up the earth's surface is broken down. Small particles produce minerals which plants need to grow.

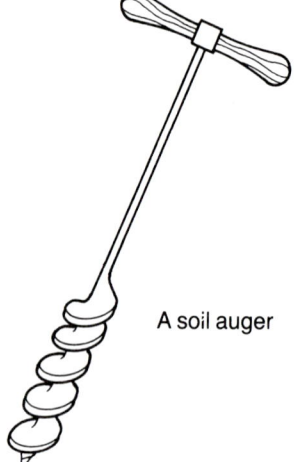

A soil auger

Texture

The texture or 'feel' of a soil depends on the size of the rock particles it contains.

Experiment Feel the soil in your hands and decide whether the soil is:

1 SANDY SOIL – this will feel coarse and gritty to touch. It contains little humus. Water drains through easily.

2 CLAY SOIL – will feel smooth to the touch. It is sticky when wet. It is easily rolled into a ball. It is often very wet and difficult to dig. When it is dry it is very hard. It contains plenty of humus.

3 LOAM – neither of the above, it is silky to the touch. It clings to the hand. It is well drained but keeps enough water for plants. It is easy to dig. It contains humus.

Decide which the type of soil is from the following:

SANDY – SANDY LOAM – LOAM – CLAYEY LOAM – CLAY

A record kept on a chart like this will help you decide.

SOIL SAMPLE	ROUGH	SMOOTH	DRY	STICKY	PLASTIC	GRITTY	SOIL TYPE
A		✔	✔		✔		Loam
B							
C							
D							

HUMUS
Rotted vegetation and animal waste

ACIDITY
The level of acid in the soil

Depth

Plant roots grow better in a deeper soil.

Method

You will need a soil auger and a large sheet of paper.

1 Use a soil auger to bring a sample of soil from as deep as possible.

2 Take a piece of soil from all levels on the auger.

3 Rub each piece on a large sheet of paper at the level it was taken from the auger.

4 Look for where the layers change from lighter to darker.
Draw a line across the paper.

5 Try to mark other layers.

6 Compare charts from each site
– The darker layer is the humus
– The lighter layer is less fertile.
A deep humus layer is best for the garden.

Acidity

Different minerals in the soil can give it different levels of acidity. Plants like different levels of acidity. Some, like hydrangeas, change the colour of their flowers depending on the level of acidity in the soil. Most plants like a neutral soil. The acid in the soil can be changed by using chemicals.

Experiment

What we need to measure acidity
- Cork
- Test tube
- Distilled water
- Soil indicator
- Barium sulphate powder
- An acid colour chart

1 Into the test tube place
(a) 2½ cm of soil (take out the roots and stones)
(b) Barium sulphate powder
   1cm for sandy soil
   2cm for loam
   3cm for clay
   to break up soil particles
(c) Distilled water (⅔ way up tube)
(d) A few drops of soil indicator

2 Place cork into top of tube and shake vigorously.

3 Allow to settle. Match with acidity level chart to find pH acidity value.

4 Make a graph like this of values of soil acidity
(pH Value 0–12, Site A, Site B, Site C, Site D)

To find out which site has the best soil for the garden answer the following questions.

4 Join with a group of four or five people. Draw a recording table like the one opposite. Fill in the boxes,
either – using the results from the 'Details of the soil survey' at Carter Lodge shown opposite.
or – using the results of experiments you have done yourselves.

5 Now fill in the score boxes on the table. To do this give a mark out of 10 for each result for each site. To get 10 marks the soil has to be perfect for a garden.

6 Add up the scores for each site A, B, C, D. The site with the highest score is first. Mark the sites in order 1st, 2nd, 3rd, 4th.

Details of soil survey for the four sites at Carter Lodge School

Humus 10cm	Humus 8cm	Humus 4cm	Humus 8cm
p.H 6.0 Loam	pH 5.5 Sandy Loam	pH 5.0 Sandy Loam	pH 5.5 Clayey Loam

Recording table

Site	Soil depth		Soil texture		Soil acidity		Best soil	
	Result	Score	Result	Score	Result	Score	Total score	Order
A					PH6.0			
B					PH5.5			
C					PH5.0			
D					PH5.5			

Is there a slope?

When planning a garden it is important that the ground is reasonably flat. Sites which have steep slopes may cause difficulties in the following ways:

(a) **Soil movement** – the pull of gravity causes the soil to move slowly down a slope. This leaves only a thin layer of soil at the top of the slope.

(b) **Soil washed away** – after heavy rain the water often runs over the top of the ground. It flows down the slope carrying with it some of the soil.

(c) **Garden work** – it is hard for gardeners to work with machinery and garden tools on a steep slope.

1 The plants which grow in a garden need water.

(a) If the ground slopes will heavy or light rain be best for the plants?

(b) Give two reasons for your answer.

2 Study the diagram 'How do we measure slope angle?' and then look at the three CLINOMETERS below. What slope angle does each show?

CLINOMETER
An instrument for measuring angles

How do we measure slope angle?

For this experiment you will need a clinometer and two poles.

To make a clinometer

Trace a protractor onto a piece of card and label the angles.

Attach a piece of string to the centre and use a pencil as a weight.

When the clinometer is tipped the string shows the slope angle.

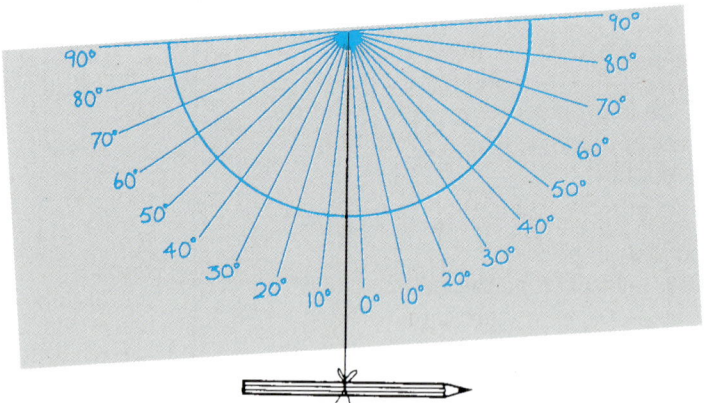

1 Place one pole into the ground at the bottom of the slope and fix the clinometer to the pole at a height of 1.5 metres.
2 At the top of the slope place the second pole into the ground with a marker at 1.5 metres on the pole.
3 Look along the straight edge of the clinometer to the marker on the other pole at the top of the slope and read off the slope angle.

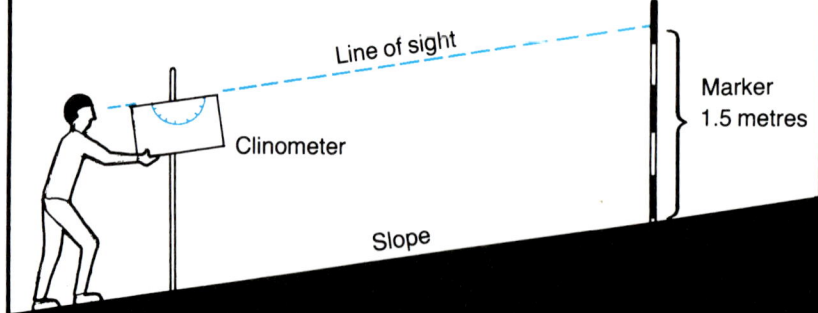

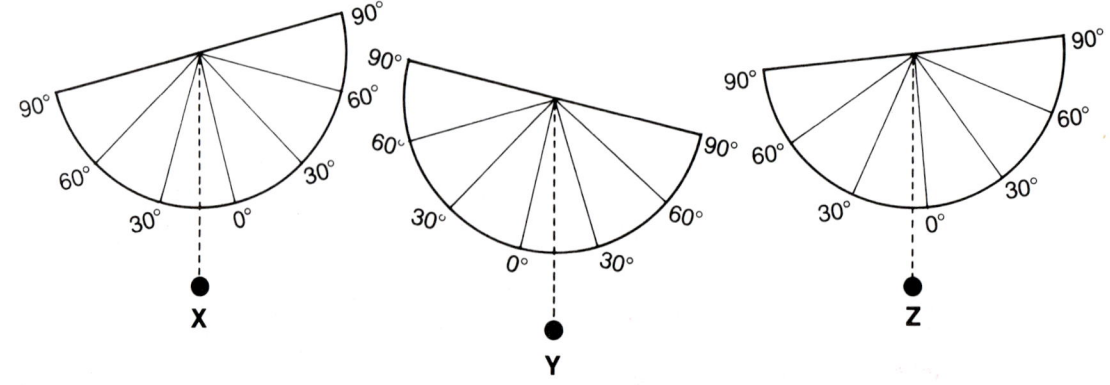

Which way does the garden face?

The direction in which the garden slopes or 'faces' is known as its ASPECT. Even if a garden is flat there may be a building or fence on one side of it. This will also be important as the garden may be shaded.

3 Put each of the sites E, F, G and H on the diagram in order from warmest to coolest.

4 Write a sentence about sites A, B, C and D at Carter Lodge School. Say whether or not each will have enough sunlight. You must look at the map on page 6. The map will tell you the positions of buildings, walls, hedges etc. These may shade the garden.

5 Use a protractor to draw the four slope angles given in the table. This will give you a better idea of the steepness of slope.

6 The arrows in the 'Aspect' column of the table show the direction each site faces. Using the compass points N, S, E and W write down the direction in which each site at Carter Lodge faces.

How do we find the aspect of a site?

In the northern HEMISPHERE the sun rises in the east, shines from the south east, south and south west and sets in the west.
In the northern hemisphere the sun never shines from the north.
The diagram shows how each ray of sun has a different amount of land to warm.
How much land the rays of sun have to warm depends on
(a) The way the slope faces
(b) The steepness of the slope

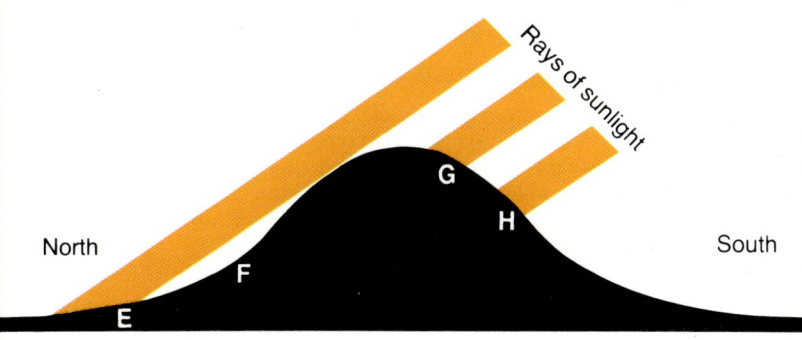

The Experiment
To find the aspect of a site use a compass to discover which direction is north. Do this at each of the possible sites for the garden. Record the direction in which each site faces.

7 Copy and complete the chart below using the information from the 'Results' table to make your choice of the best site for slope angle and aspect.

Order	1st	2nd	3rd	4th
Slope angle				
Aspect				

Results from Carter Lodge School

Site	Slope angle	Aspect
A	6°	↙ N
B	9°	↓ E–W
C	2°	← S
D	12°	→

ASPECT
The direction in which a slope faces

HEMISPHERE
A half of the world

The wind

The **direction** and **strength** of the wind can affect plants in a garden.

How to find out the direction of the wind

Using a wind vane

The direction of the wind is always given as the point **from which the wind is coming**. A wind vane shows direction. The arrow points to the direction from which the wind is coming and shows the wind direction.

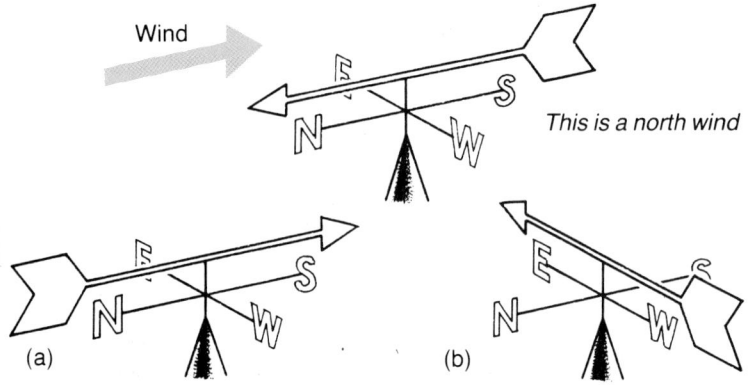

Using a paper streamer

A way of finding wind direction without using a wind vane is to use a paper streamer. Mark the points of the compass on the ground. Then hold up a streamer to find the wind direction.

The wind will be coming from behind the person holding the streamer so this will be the wind direction.

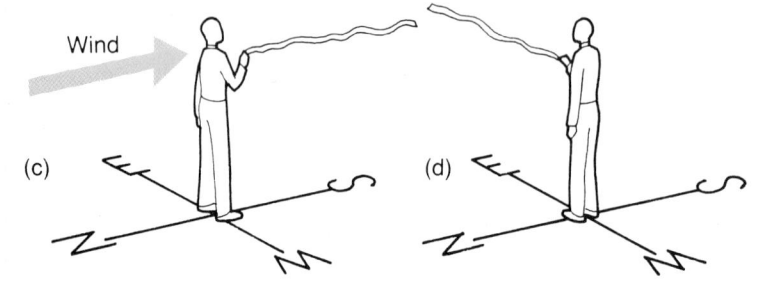

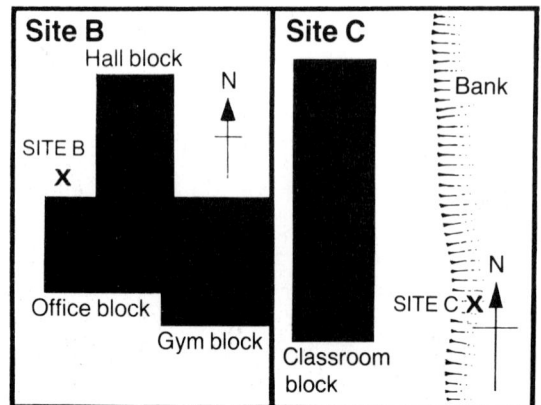

The direction of the wind

Winds from the north and east are cold. They are not welcome in a garden. The winds from the south and west are warmer. Nearby buildings may shelter a site.

1 Complete the sentences below using words chosen from this list (note that there are more words than you need):
north, south, strength, east, direction, west.
Plants in a garden may be affected by the ……… and ……… of the wind. The best site for a garden is one which is sheltered from winds from the ……… and ……… .

2 Look at the section 'How to find out the direction of the wind'.
What is the wind direction shown in diagrams (a) (b) (c) and (d)?

3 Look at the plan of site B at Carter Lodge School. This site is sheltered from winds on two sides. The office block shelters the site from winds from the south. The hall shelters the site from winds from the east.
From which wind does the classroom block shelter site C?

4 Complete the table below using the map of Carter Lodge School on page 6. Put the sites in order of best to worst for wind direction.

Site	A	B	C	D
Wind sheltered from		south and east		
Order 1st to 4th				

The strength of the wind

Strong winds can damage plants by breaking them or blowing them over.

The strength and direction of the wind can be affected by nearby buildings, trees and other obstacles. Sites quite close together may provide different recordings at the same time.

5 Using the wind strength results for Carter Lodge School add up the numbers for each site. Divide by 10 to find the average wind strength number for each site.

6 Copy and complete the table below by placing the sites in order. Use your results from the wind direction and the wind strength tables (you have already completed the order for wind direction).

	1st	2nd	3rd	4th
Wind direction				
Wind strength				
Overall order for wind				

How to find out the strength of the wind

The strength of the wind depends on its speed.
One way of finding the wind speed is to use the Beaufort Scale. This is the scale used on the Shipping forecast. By looking at smoke and trees you can find the type of wind and its speed.

Beaufort Scale

Beaufort Number	Type of wind	Observation	Speed (km/hr)
0	Calm	Smoke rises vertically	–
1	Light air	Smoke drifts	1–6
2	Light breeze	Leaves rustle	7–12
3	Gentle breeze	Leaves move	13–18
4	Moderate breeze	Small branches move	19–30
5	Fresh breeze	Small trees sway a little	31–40
6	Strong breeze	Large branches sway	41–51
7	Moderate gale	Whole trees sway	52–60
8	Fresh gale	Twigs break off trees	61–74
9	Strong gale	Large branches blown down	75–86
10	Whole gale	Trees uprooted	87–100

However this is difficult to use for small sites. The wind speed may change in places quite close to each other. This happens when one place is sheltered. In these cases we can use an instrument to tell us the wind speed. Two instruments which could be used are an anemometer and a wind speed vane.

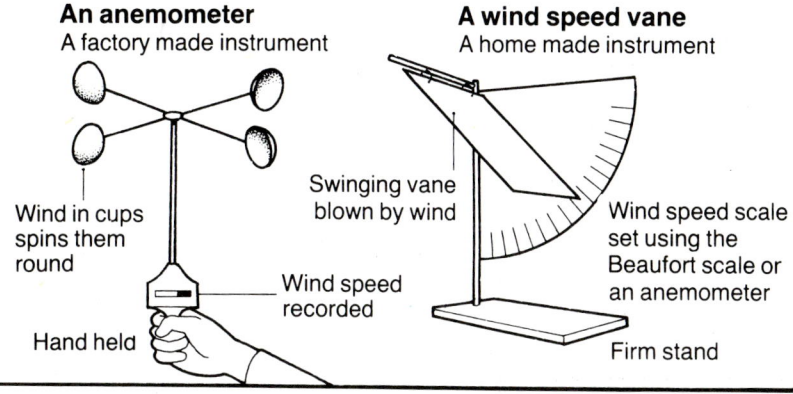

An anemometer — A factory made instrument
Wind in cups spins them round. Hand held. Wind speed recorded.

A wind speed vane — A home made instrument
Swinging vane blown by wind. Wind speed scale set using the Beaufort scale or an anemometer. Firm stand.

The wind strength (speed) results for Carter Lodge School
(observations over 10 days) (Km/hr)

Day	1	2	3	4	5	6	7	8	9	10
SPEED SITE A	0	0	4	4	4	14	26	8	5	5
SPEED SITE B	0	0	2	3	5	10	20	4	3	3
SPEED SITE C	0	0	4	4	6	16	30	10	6	4
SPEED SITE D	0	0	4	6	6	12	24	8	5	5

Temperature

Temperature is important when choosing a site for a garden. If the site is too cold the plants will not grow as quickly or as well. Quite different temperatures can be found at different sites on the same day.

Temperature is very closely linked with **aspect**. Is the site facing the sun or is it in the shadow of trees or a building?

Temperature is also very closely linked with **wind speed** and **wind direction**. Is the site sheltered from the wind?

How to measure air temperature

We use a thermometer to measure air temperature. Hold the top of the thermometer about 1.5 metres above the ground. Wait until the temperature level is steady. Then take a reading and record it. Measure the temperature at each end of the site.

1 Copy the following sentences and choose the correct word from the brackets.
(a) A site facing north is (cooler/warmer) than a site facing south.
(b) The suns rays (reach/do not reach) a site facing north.

2 Copy the following sentence and choose the correct word from the brackets.
(a) The temperature at each site is more likely to be different on a (windy/calm) day.
(b) Copy and complete this sentence. The reason for my choice of word is …
....

3 Draw a bar graph to show differences in temperature for the four sites at Carter Lodge School.

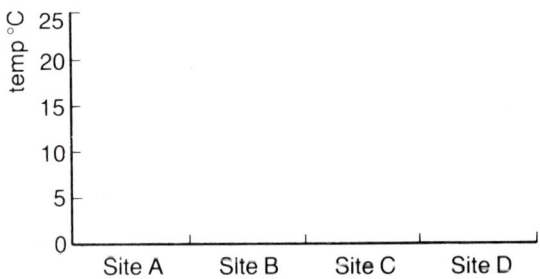

4 Put the sites in order 1st, 2nd, 3rd or 4th for temperature.

Results for Carter Lodge School		
	Temperature °C	Comments on site
Site A	19	Quite exposed, very little shelter receives plenty of sunlight.
Site B	18	Sheltered by buildings but exposed to westerley winds. Part of the area permanently shaded.
Site C	19	Sheltered by buildings and bushes, these also block sunlight for several hours per day.
Site D	19	Quite exposed to winds but does receive maximum sunlight.

Human activity

There is one last thing we have to consider. We need to look at the present use of the sites. We must try and choose a site which will not cause disturbance to other activities.

We also have to choose a site which will not cost too much to change into a garden.

We should also check on the usage of the area at break and lunchtimes.

Results of human activity survey for Carter Lodge School

Site	Present use	No. of pupils at break	No. of pupils at lunchtime	Any future plans	Best site 1st 2nd 3rd 4th
A	Disused, remains of part of an old greenhouse, disused garden area.	10	4	Likely to be extension of school car park.	
B	Ornamental grassed area near main school entrance and head teacher's study.	0	0	None	
C	Top section of school sports field, close to long jump pit.	36	52	Could be a works area for extension to D block. This could affect small part of the proposed garden.	
D	Lower section of school playing field close to soccer pitch.	2	8	None	

The final decision

Where should the garden be located?

5 Join with others in a group. Make a table like the one below. Fill in all the RANK ORDERS you have completed. Use the table and all the other information you have collected to decide where the garden should be sited. Talk with other groups about why you chose your site.

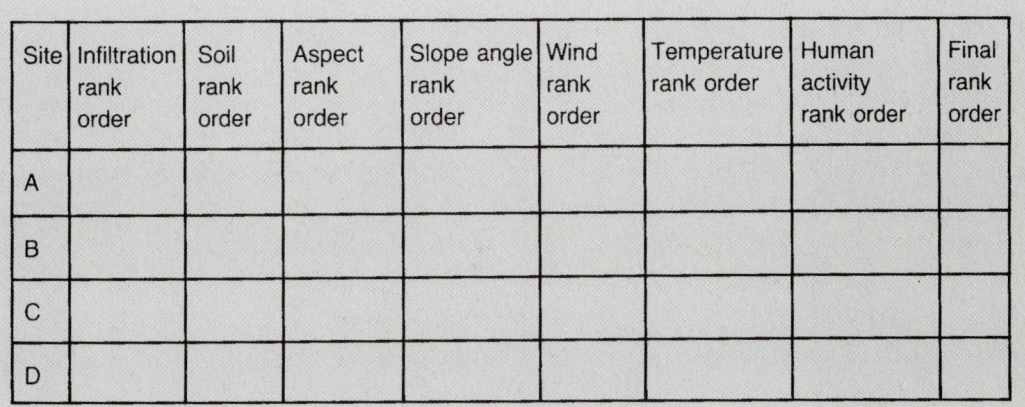

RANK ORDER
Placing things in order from best to worst or first to last

Site	Infiltration rank order	Soil rank order	Aspect rank order	Slope angle rank order	Wind rank order	Temperature rank order	Human activity rank order	Final rank order
A								
B								
C								
D								

Decision – the best site is?

Unit 2 VALLEYS

The Shirebrook
Can we improve the environment?

The Shirebrook is a river which flows through part of south east Sheffield. It is a TRIBUTARY of the River Rother. In the past two hundred years there have been many changes in the valley. The area used to be countryside. Most of the land was used for farming. There was also an old FORGE in the valley. The people of Hackenthorpe were mostly farmers. The villagers of Beighton and Woodhouse worked in the mines.

The biggest change came to the valley in the 1950s. Sheffield grew in size. Sheffield built large housing estates at Frecheville and Hackenthorpe.

The photograph shows some of the present day land uses. They can be seen in and around the Shirebrook Valley.

Sheffield City Council want to improve the Shirebrook Valley. The Council plan to make the valley a park. We shall look at some of these ideas in more detail.

The Shirebrook looking North

TRIBUTARY
A small river which flows into a larger river

FORGE
A workshop where a blacksmith made things out of iron

18

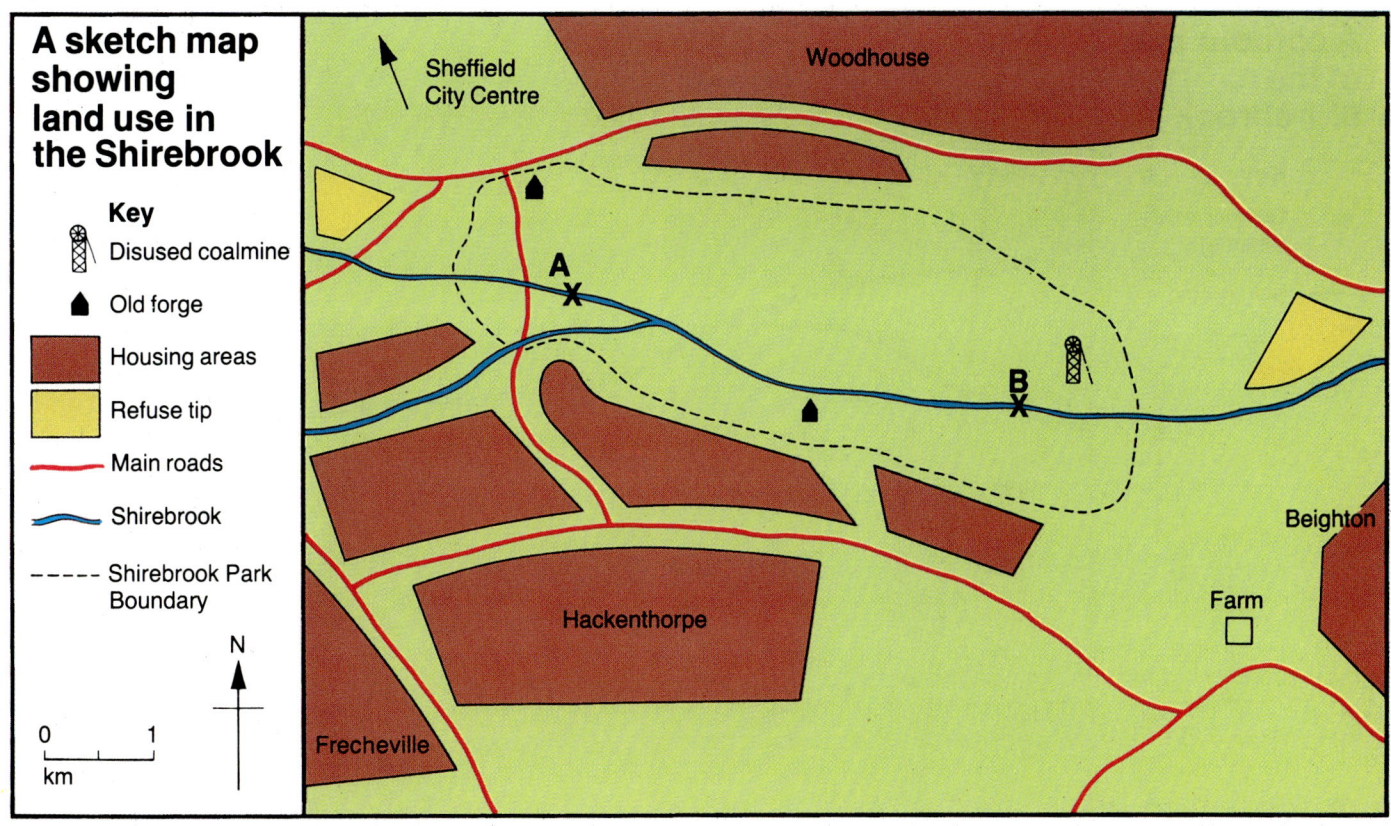

The task

Our task is to try to improve the environment of the Shirebrook Valley. To do this we are going to build a small boating lake. People can relax and have picnics at the side of the lake. We will LANDSCAPE the area. To do this we will make flower beds. We will plant trees and have grassed areas.

There are two places where the boating lake could be. We have to choose which place is best for the lake. The picnic site will be around the lake.

1 Think about what you have read about the Shirebrook Valley.
(a) Describe the location of the Shirebrook Valley.
(b) Write about what the area was like before 1950.

2 Read the information and look at the map of the Shirebrook Valley. Make a list to describe some of the present day land uses.

3 Inside the new Shirebrook Park is a disused coal-mine. Complete the following:
To make the coal-mine more attractive I would ....
....

4 The Park could be made more interesting to visit.
FEATURES could be made or built in the Park. Complete the following:
To make the Park more interesting I would

(a) ....
(b) ....
(c) ....

TO LANDSCAPE
To change the shape and appearance of an area of land to make it more attractive

FEATURES
Things of special interest in an area

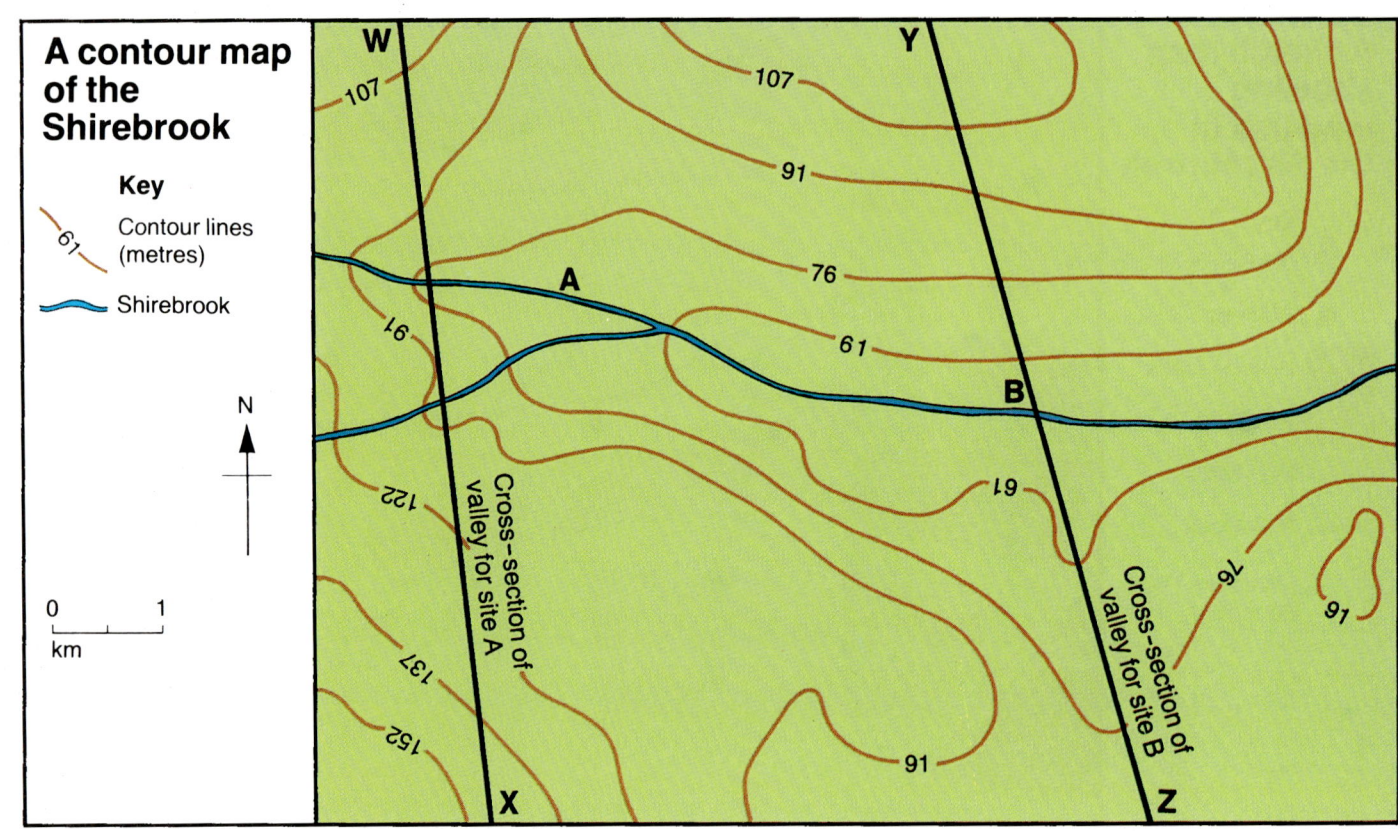

A contour map of the Shirebrook

Key
— Contour lines (metres)
— Shirebrook

This map shows the RELIEF of the Shirebrook Valley. Two lines are drawn across the Valley: W – X and Y – Z. They are the lines of the CROSS-SECTIONS shown on the opposite page. The points where they cross the river are the two possible sites for the boating lake.

RELIEF
The shape of the land. How flat or hilly an area is. How steep or gentle the slopes are

CROSS-SECTION
A picture which is cut through to show a side view

1 (a) If you walked from point A to point B, how far would you have travelled?

(b) In which direction would you have been walking?

(c) Would you be walking uphill or downhill?

2 Look at the contour map. Describe the relief of the land in this area. (Remember: if contour lines are close together the slopes are steeper. If contour lines are more spaced out slopes are gentler.)

3 Look at the two cross-sections of the Valley to help you to complete these sentences.

(a) At site A the river is ____ metres above sea level.

(b) At site B the river is ____ metres above sea level.

(c) Between sites A and B the river has fallen ____ metres.

4 Which site would you choose as the best site for the boating lake? Look at the two cross-sections to help you. Give a reason for your answer.

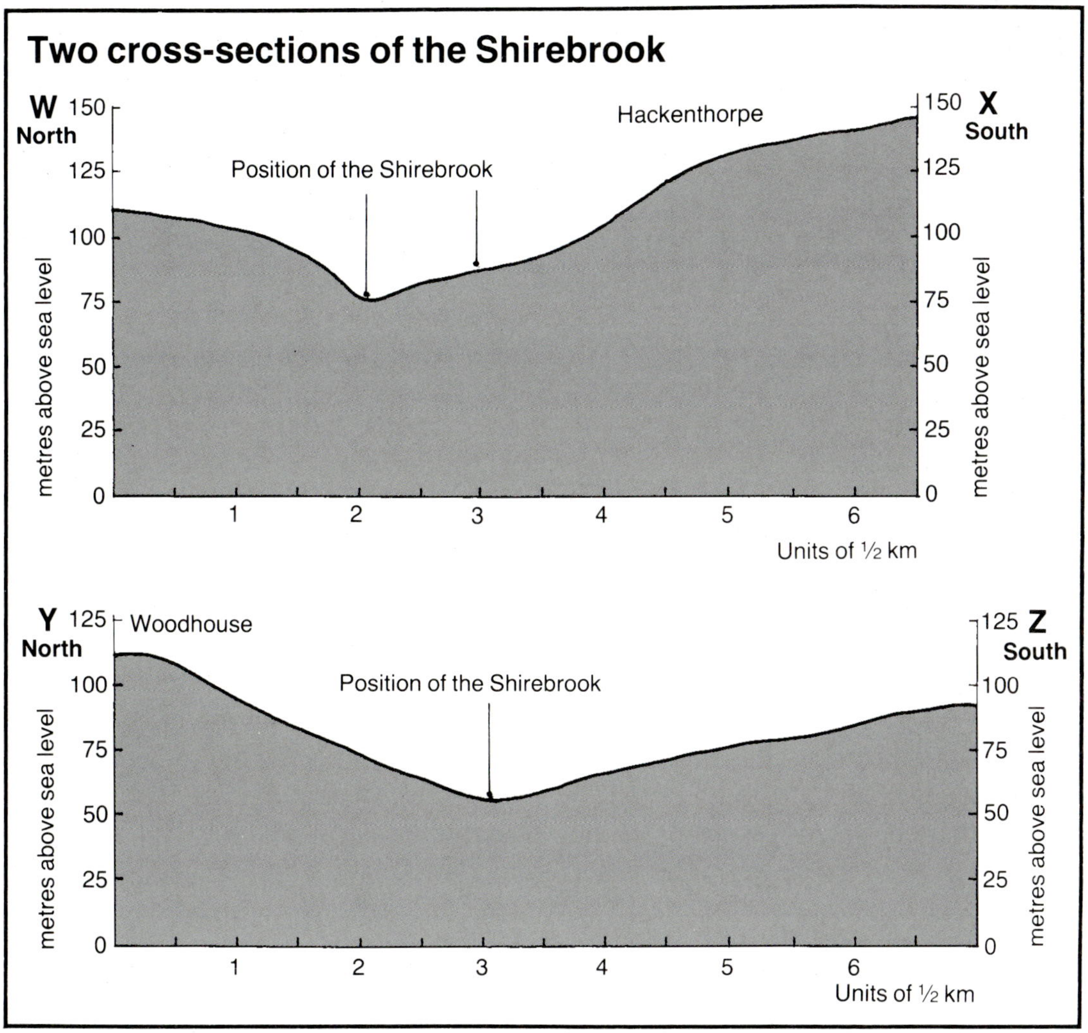

Two cross-sections of the Shirebrook

W 150 North — Hackenthorpe — 150 X South
(metres above sea level)
Position of the Shirebrook
Units of ½ km

Y 125 North — Woodhouse — 125 Z South
Position of the Shirebrook
Units of ½ km

A boating lake

As well as making the Shirebrook cleaner and more attractive, Sheffield City Council are going to use the land in the valley for other purposes. Some of the land which is not used at the moment will become farmland. The bottom of the valley is often very wet and could be used for grazing, whilst the valley sides could be planted with crops.

The old forge is also going to be rebuilt in its original state close to point A.

5 Sheffield City Council would like to make space for farmland in the valley. Which side of the valley would be best? Think back to Unit 1.

6 What might the forge be used for when it is rebuilt?

How was the valley formed?

For thousands of years the Shirebrook river has cut down into the land to make the valley.

The running water flows over the land. The water washes away sand, silt and sometimes bigger pieces of stone. These are washed away by EROSION from the BED and BANKS of the river.

The amount of erosion depends on how fast the water is flowing. In the summer there is much less water in the stream. It flows very slowly. The water will remove very little sand, SILT, or stones.

In the winter the river has much more water. It flows faster. The banks and bed are more likely to be worn away by erosion.

Where water flows slowly it cannot carry large pieces of rock, gravel and sand. These are DEPOSITED by the river. The bed and banks of part of the Shirebrook river are of sand, gravel and silt. The sand, gravel and silt are known as ALLUVIUM.

1 Water wears away the river bed and banks. In winter there is more wearing away. In summer there is less wearing away of the river bed and banks. Explain why this happens.

BED
The base of the river

BANKS
The edges of the river, where the water meets land

EROSION
The wearing away and removal of rock by water, ice or wind

SILT
Fine particles of material carried or deposited by the river

DEPOSITED
Material left behind by the river, e.g. sand, stones

ALLUVIUM
Material deposited by a stream or river

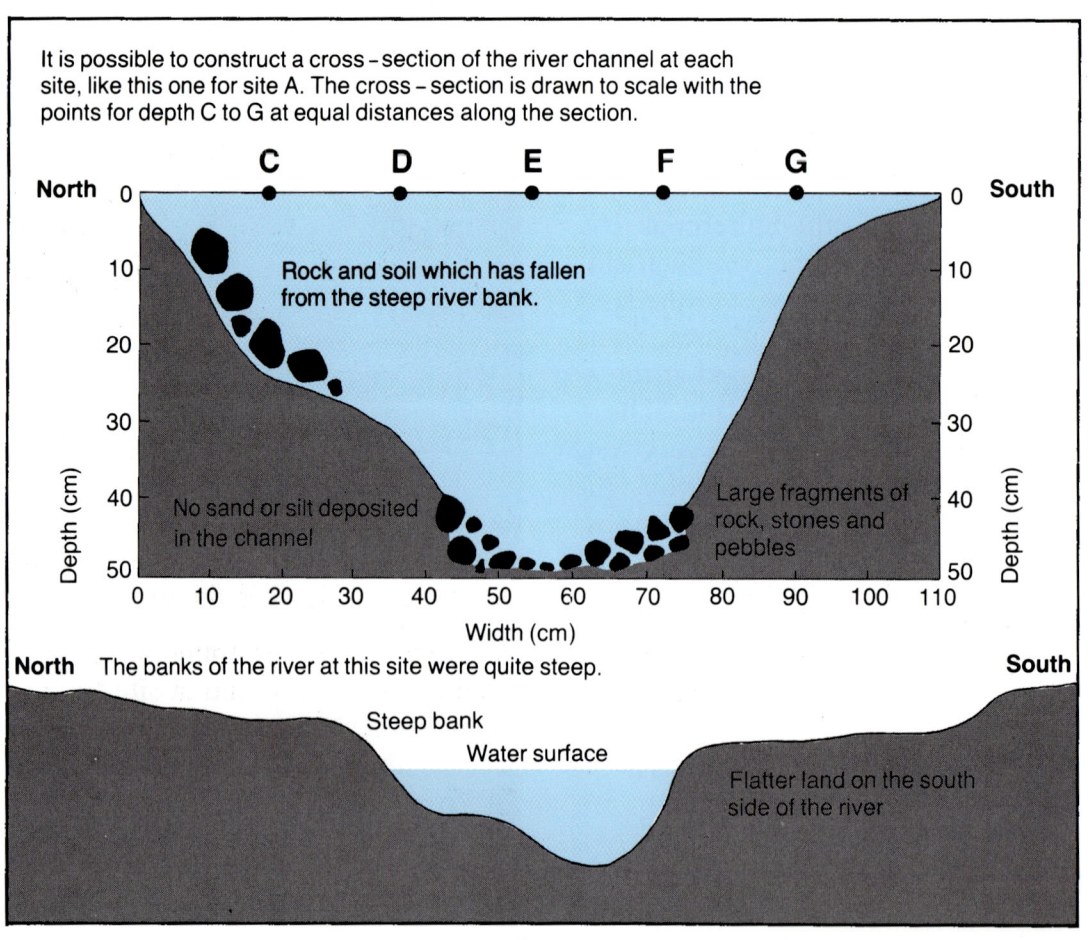

2 (a) Using the figures for site B draw a cross-section of the river channel. Use a framework like the one used in the cross-section for site A.

(b) The features on the photograph are labelled. Write these labels on your cross-section to show the same features.

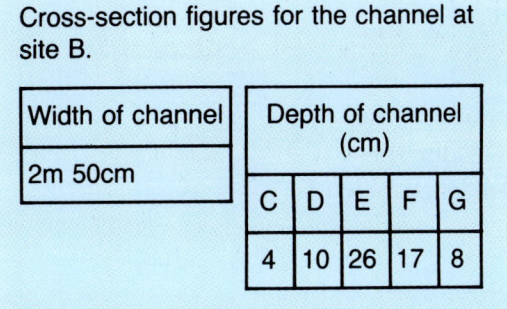

Cross-section figures for the channel at site B.

Width of channel	Depth of channel (cm)				
2m 50cm	C	D	E	F	G
	4	10	26	17	8

Flatter land at the side of the stream

Small rock fragments on the stream bed covered with sand and silt

Gentle river banks

River channel at site B

3 Site A and B river channels and banks are different. List three differences between sites A and B.

The speed of the water at sites A and B was measured. The pupils marked out 10 metres along the bank. They dropped a cork in the water and timed how long it took to travel 10 metres. They did this ten times at each site. They worked out their AVERAGE. Here are their results
Site A   2.2 seconds per metre
Site B   4.6 seconds per metre

Smaller rock fragments of silt and sand were found in the river bed at site B. Only larger rock fragments are found at site A. The slower flowing water did not have the power to remove even the smallest particles at site B.

4 (a) Silt builds up at site B. This might be a problem for a boating lake. What do you think is the problem?

(b) Larger rocks are found at site A. Smaller rocks are found at site B. Why are larger rocks found at site A?

5 There are two sites, A and B. Which site is the best for a boating lake? Discuss your choice with a friend.

AVERAGE
Add up all the times and divide by ten

1 Look at the photograph of the site you have chosen.

(a) Copy the table opposite.

(b) Decide how you feel about the view. Then place a tick under the score you have chosen for each pair of words on the table.

(c) Add up the final score. What does this tell you about the way you feel for the site?

2 Use the photograph for the site you have chosen.

(a) Make a drawing of how the area would look after the boating lake had been built and the landscaping had taken place.

(b) Label the drawing clearly. The labels will show your plans and ideas.

3 Carry out a survey of your drawing. To do this:

(a) Copy the table above.

(b) Look at your drawing. Decide how you feel about the view.

(c) Place a tick under the headings 1, 2, 3, 4, or 5.

(d) Add up the final score.

(e) Compare the final score for the photograph with the final score for the drawing. What do you notice?

Sheffield City Council are tidying up and improving the environment. Council Planners have had ideas about the Shirebrook. The ideas are listed on the opposite page in a booklet made by the Council.

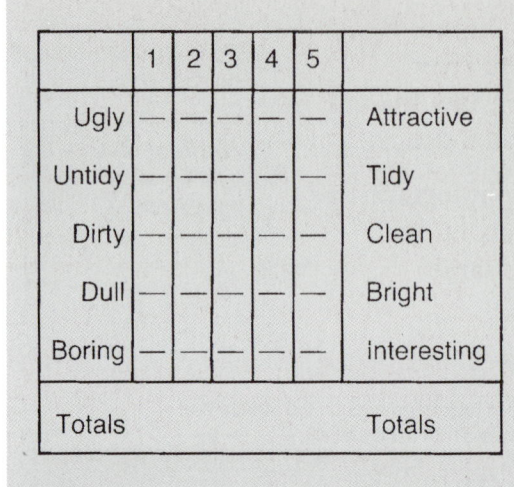

	1	2	3	4	5	
Ugly	—	—	—	—	—	Attractive
Untidy	—	—	—	—	—	Tidy
Dirty	—	—	—	—	—	Clean
Dull	—	—	—	—	—	Bright
Boring	—	—	—	—	—	interesting
Totals						Totals

Final score =

The landscape at site A

The landscape at site B

- New farm land
- Clearing the water in the stream
- Clearing the banks of the stream
- Large scale tree planting
- Improving the appearance of the INDUSTRIAL ESTATE
- RENOVATE the old forge
- New playing fields
- Improving footpaths
- A new road
- Picnic sites
- Clean out the forge dam and stock with fish

Improving the Shirebrook

Would you like to live in an area where a brook flows through fields and woodlands; a haven for birds, wild animals and flowers; where footpaths lead you through attractive countryside; an area for walking, horse riding, fishing as well as football and children's play areas?

INDUSTRIAL ESTATE
A large area of land with small, modern factories built on it

RENOVATE
Improving the quality of an area by landscaping and rebuilding

Choosing the site

Site	Advantages	Disadvantages
A		
B		

Join with others in a group and look at the information on this page. A small boating lake is to be built. You are going to choose the best site. To help you decide:
(a) Make a big drawing of the table.
(b) Answer the questions below. Put your answers under Advantages and Disadvantages.

* Which site would fill with water most easily?
* Which site would have most deposition?
* Which site would suffer from material SLUMPING into it?
* Which site could most easily be dammed?
* Which site would have the flattest land close to the banks for a picnic spot?
* Which site is most ACCESSIBLE?
* Which site would have least interference from other land uses?

SLUMPING
Material which falls into the river under gravity. Usually happens after the erosion of steep banks

ACCESSIBLE
Which point is easiest to get to by car, walking etc.

Decision – the best site is?

Unit 3: FLOODS

A natural hazard

When rivers become too full of water they may overflow and flood the land around them. Flooding causes damage to property and problems for people living in the area. For the past 350 years flood levels have been recorded on walls and buildings close to the River Ouse in York.

What causes floods?

Floods take place usually after heavy rainfall. Water running over the land surface and underground begins to fill streams and rivers. If the rain keeps falling, rivers can flow over their banks and flood the low lying area around them.

In winter snow falls and collects in the hills. If the snow melts suddenly it quickly fills the TRIBUTARY rivers which take the water to the Ouse.

Also in winter, lower temperatures mean that less water is EVAPORATED. Trees and plants use less water in winter compared to summer. This leaves more water in rivers and streams in winter and early spring.

Flood levels recorded on a wall

TRIBUTARY
A small river which flows into a larger river

EVAPORATED
Water which turns to vapour when heated by the sun. A kettle produces vapour or steam when it boils

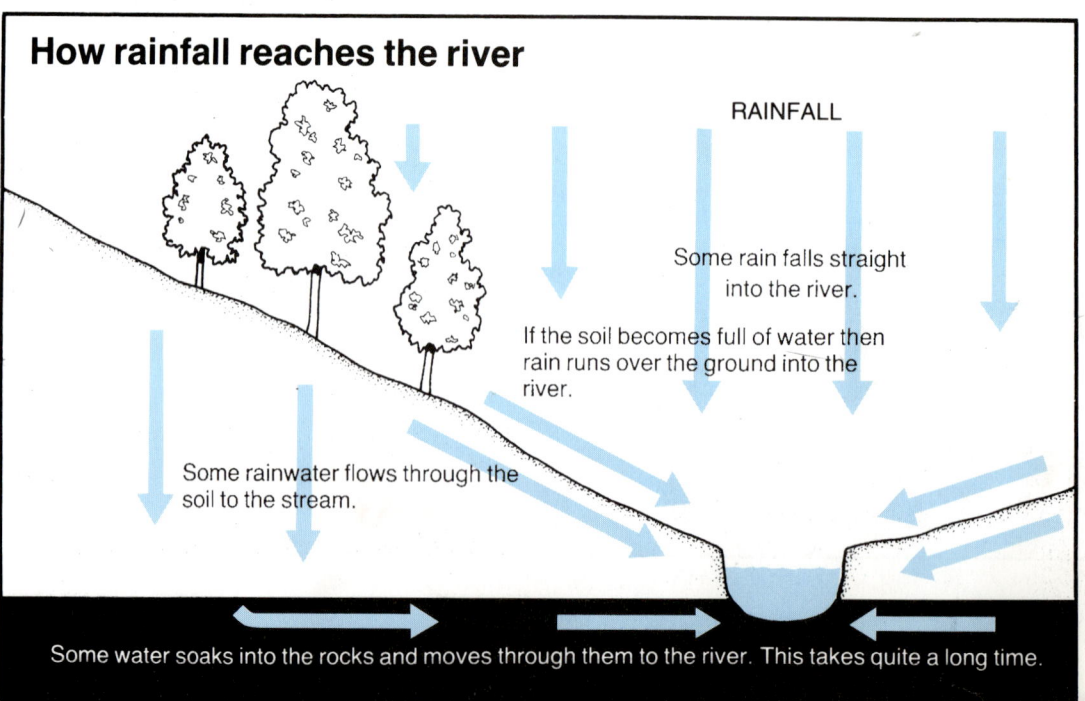

How rainfall reaches the river

Look at the map of the location of York.

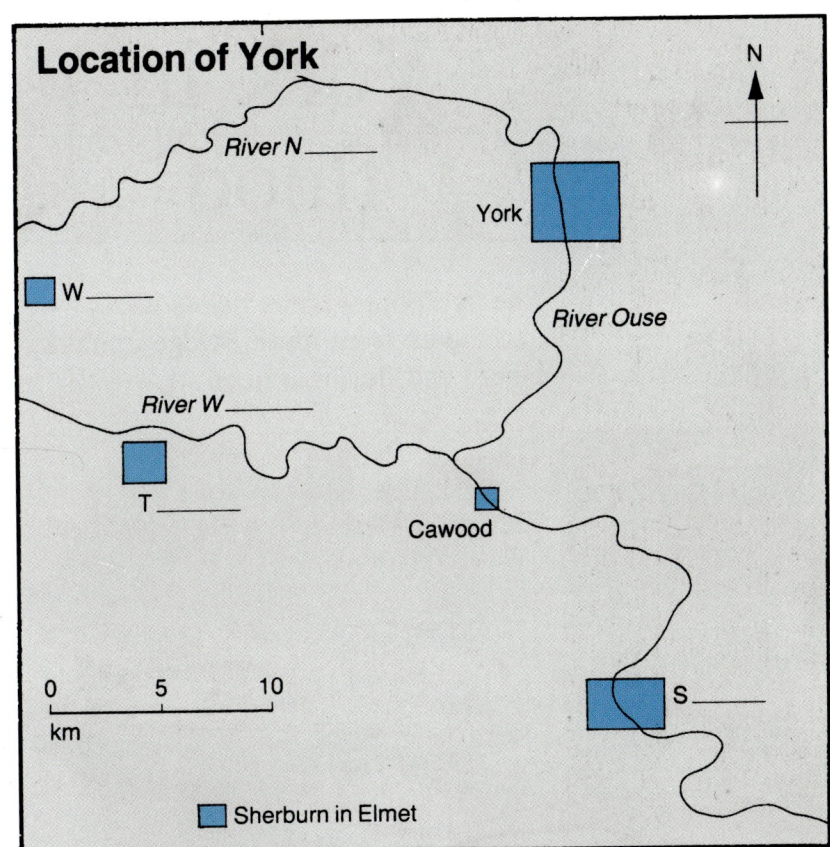

1 Use an atlas to help you find towns W, T, R, S and the rivers W and N.

2 Look at an atlas map of the North of England.
(a) Find the name of the hills where the tributaries of the Ouse start.

(b) Write down the names of four tributaries of the Ouse.

3 Look at the diagram 'How rainfall reaches the river'. Now fill in the missing words to complete these sentences:
(a) There are .... ways of rainfall reaching the river.

(b) The quickest way for water to reach the river is ....

(c) The longest way for water to reach the river is ....

4 Look at the photograph of flood levels recorded on the wall.
(a) How high was the flood level in 1625?

(b) How high was the flood level in 1947?

(c) How much higher was the water in 1625 than in 1947?

5 Why is there a risk of flooding after a heavy snowfall in winter?

6 The graph of flood levels in York shows the height of the river in metres above normal water level. If the river is 3.8 metres above the normal level it is said to be in flood. Make a list of the years when the River Ouse flooded.

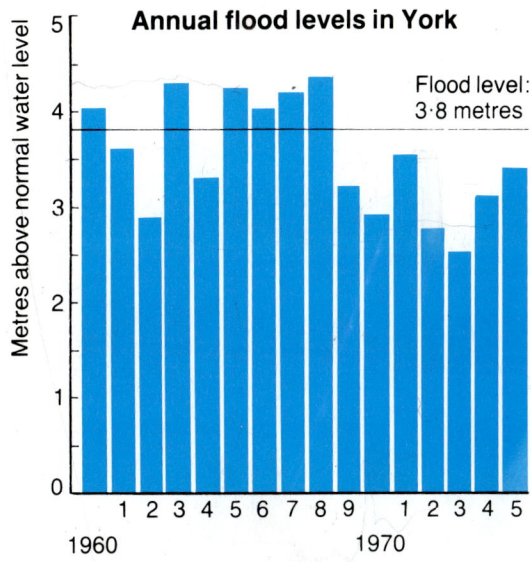

7 The following figures are water heights for 1976–1984.
Draw a bar graph like the one above to show the water levels. Give your graph a clear title.

1976 4.0 m	**1979** 4.2 m	**1982** 5.1 m
1977 3.9 m	**1980** 4.0 m	**1983** 3.0 m
1978 4.9 m	**1981** 4.1 m	**1984** 4.0 m

In which year was there not a flood?

York in flood

The two photographs below were both taken from Ouse Bridge in York, before and during a flood.

1 What has happened to the water level in the river in the bottom photograph?

2 The King's Head still opens for business during a flood but what could the owners of the public house do to stop the floods causing too much damage?

3 Look at the temperature and rainfall graph.
(a) Which month had the highest rainfall?

(b) Which month had the highest temperature?

(c) Which month had the lowest temperature?

(d) Which months are likely to have snowfall?

(e) Which months are likely to have most evaporation?

River Ouse from Ouse Bridge (top left) and River Ouse in flood from Ouse Bridge (bottom left)

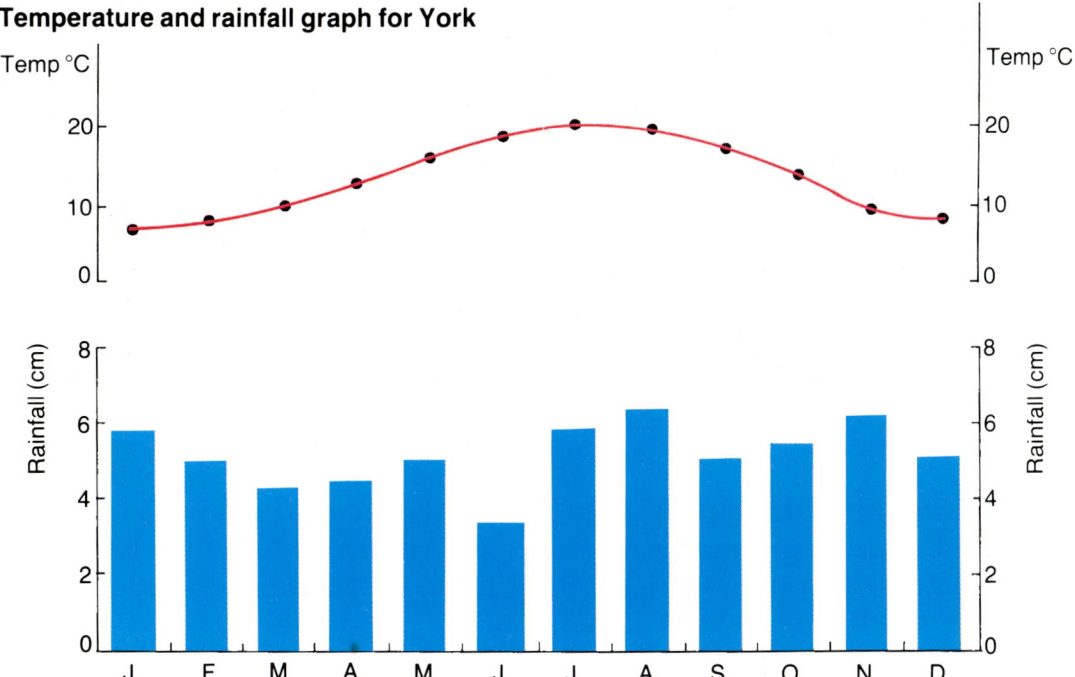

Temperature and rainfall graph for York

4 Find climate figures for your local town or area and draw a temperature and rainfall graph like the one above. You should use squared paper (graph paper).

5 Using the graph above (and the one of your local area if drawn) write a sentence to describe which season of the year floods are most likely to take place. Give reasons for your answer.

6 Look at the list of 'Floods in York'.
Imagine you lived and worked close to the River Ouse during any of these floods. Answer these questions to help you describe what happened during the flood. How did you prepare for the flood? How fast did the water rise? Did the water come into your house? Did it damage your property? Could you still get to work? Could the shops near the river stay open? How long did the water stay?

7 Make a tracing of the bottom photograph on page 28. Label your tracing to show the flooded buildings, the abandoned car, the faster water flow, and possible damage to buildings.

Floods in York. Some which have made history!

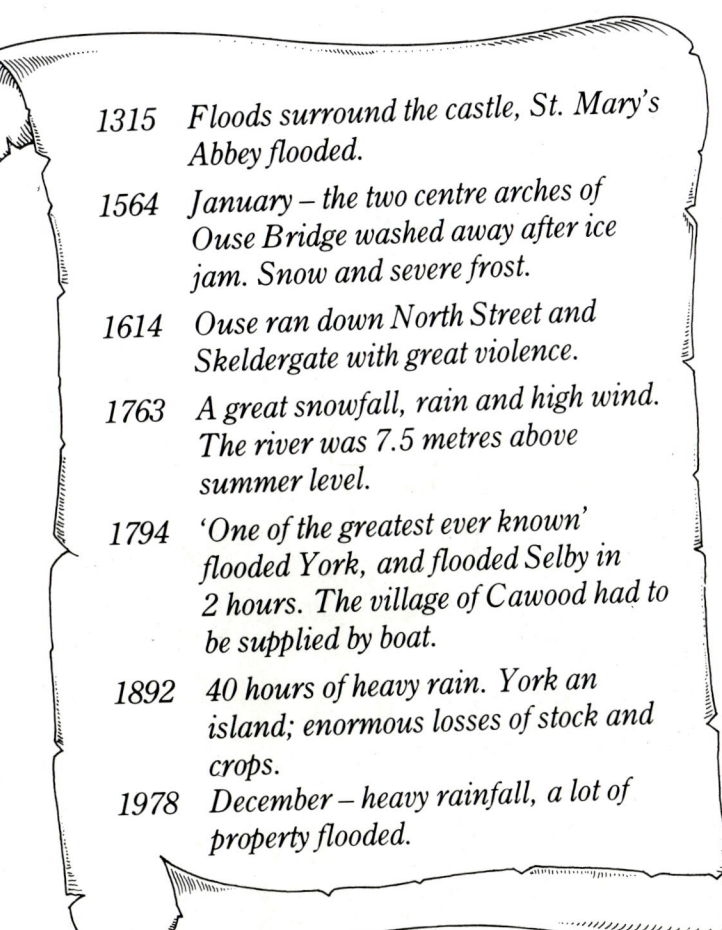

1315	Floods surround the castle, St. Mary's Abbey flooded.
1564	January – the two centre arches of Ouse Bridge washed away after ice jam. Snow and severe frost.
1614	Ouse ran down North Street and Skeldergate with great violence.
1763	A great snowfall, rain and high wind. The river was 7.5 metres above summer level.
1794	'One of the greatest ever known' flooded York, and flooded Selby in 2 hours. The village of Cawood had to be supplied by boat.
1892	40 hours of heavy rain. York an island; enormous losses of stock and crops.
1978	December – heavy rainfall, a lot of property flooded.

How to stop floods

It is the job of the Yorkshire Water Authority to stop flooding in York. For many years they have tried different FLOOD PROTECTION SCHEMES to protect the city.

The illustrations on the opposite page show some ideas which have been tried. There are four main types of protection which can be used:
1 Reinforced concrete wall
2 Mass concrete wall
3 Flood protection banks
4 Ornamental wall.

1 (a) Trace the map on this page.
(b) Colour the rivers dark blue.
(c) Colour the flooded area light blue.
(d) Colour the built up area red.

2 It is possible to work out the area of land flooded in the city by the River Ouse and the River Foss in 1982.
(a) Place your tracing paper over a piece of squared graph paper.
(b) Count the number of squares (4 mm²) inside the city covered by the flood (light blue area). **Note** that 100 squares are equal to 1 square km.
(c) Use the guide below to find how much land inside the city boundary is covered by the flood.

$$\frac{\text{Squares counted}}{100} = \ldots \text{ sq km}$$

FLOOD PROTECTION SCHEME
Holding back, or draining off water to stop flooding of a town or area

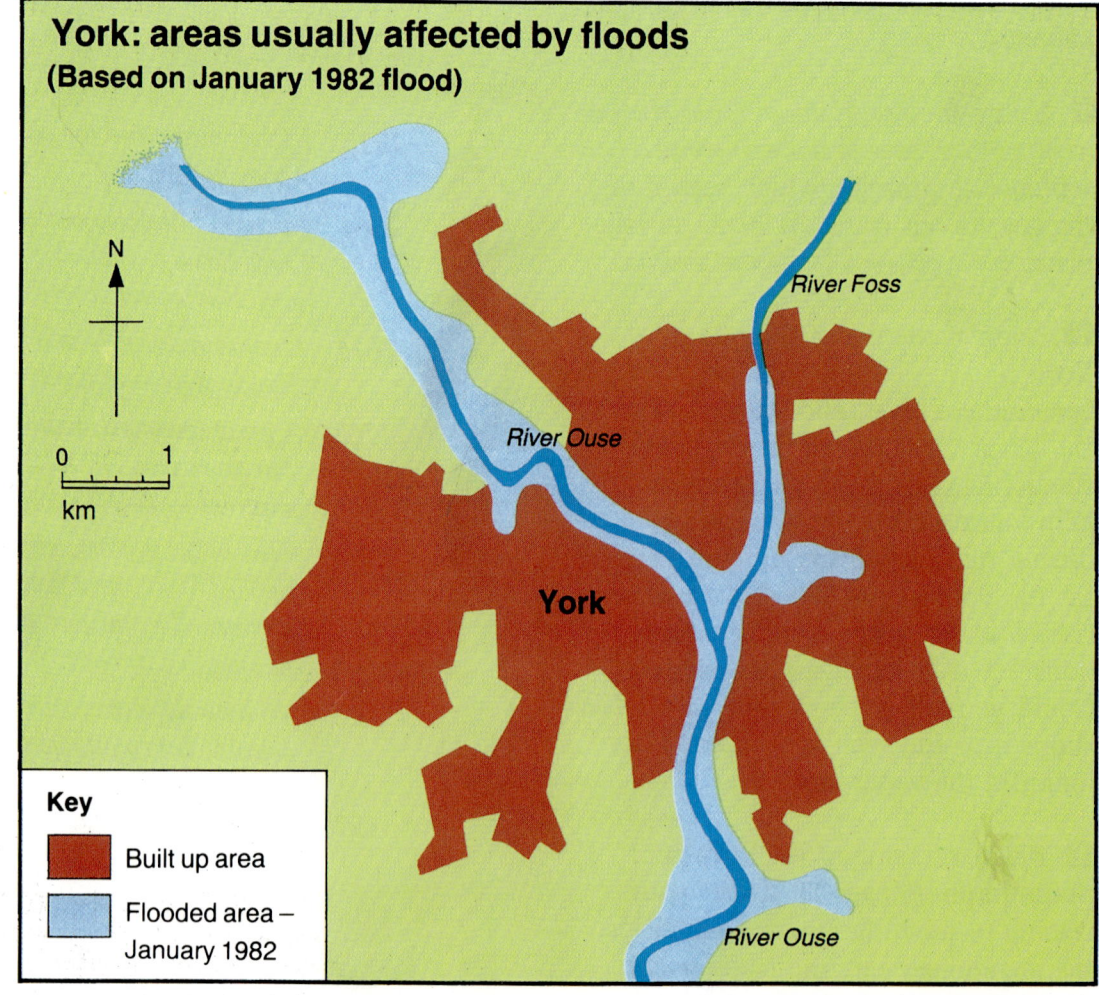

York: areas usually affected by floods (Based on January 1982 flood)

Key:
- Built up area
- Flooded area – January 1982

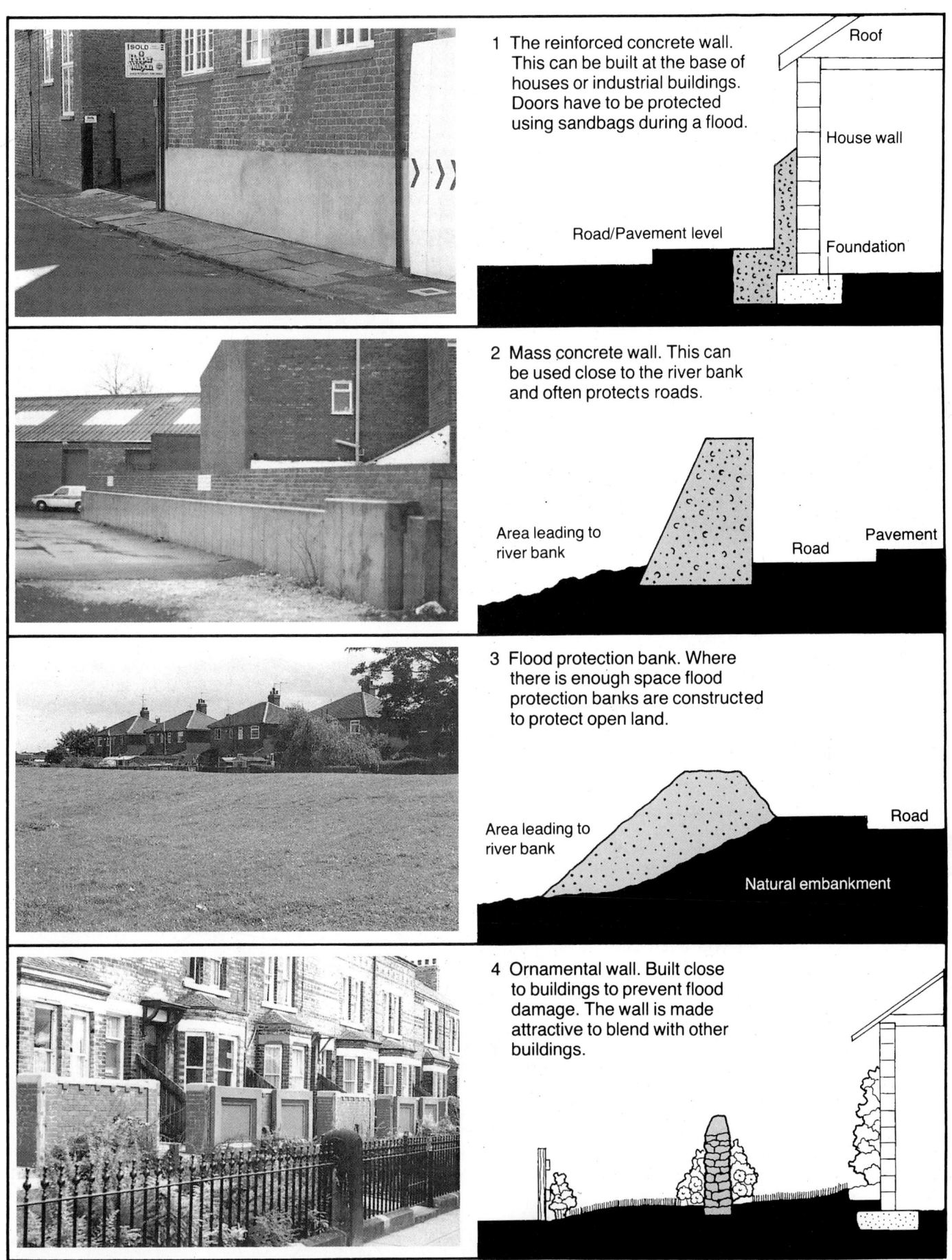

1. The reinforced concrete wall. This can be built at the base of houses or industrial buildings. Doors have to be protected using sandbags during a flood.

2. Mass concrete wall. This can be used close to the river bank and often protects roads.

3. Flood protection bank. Where there is enough space flood protection banks are constructed to protect open land.

4. Ornamental wall. Built close to buildings to prevent flood damage. The wall is made attractive to blend with other buildings.

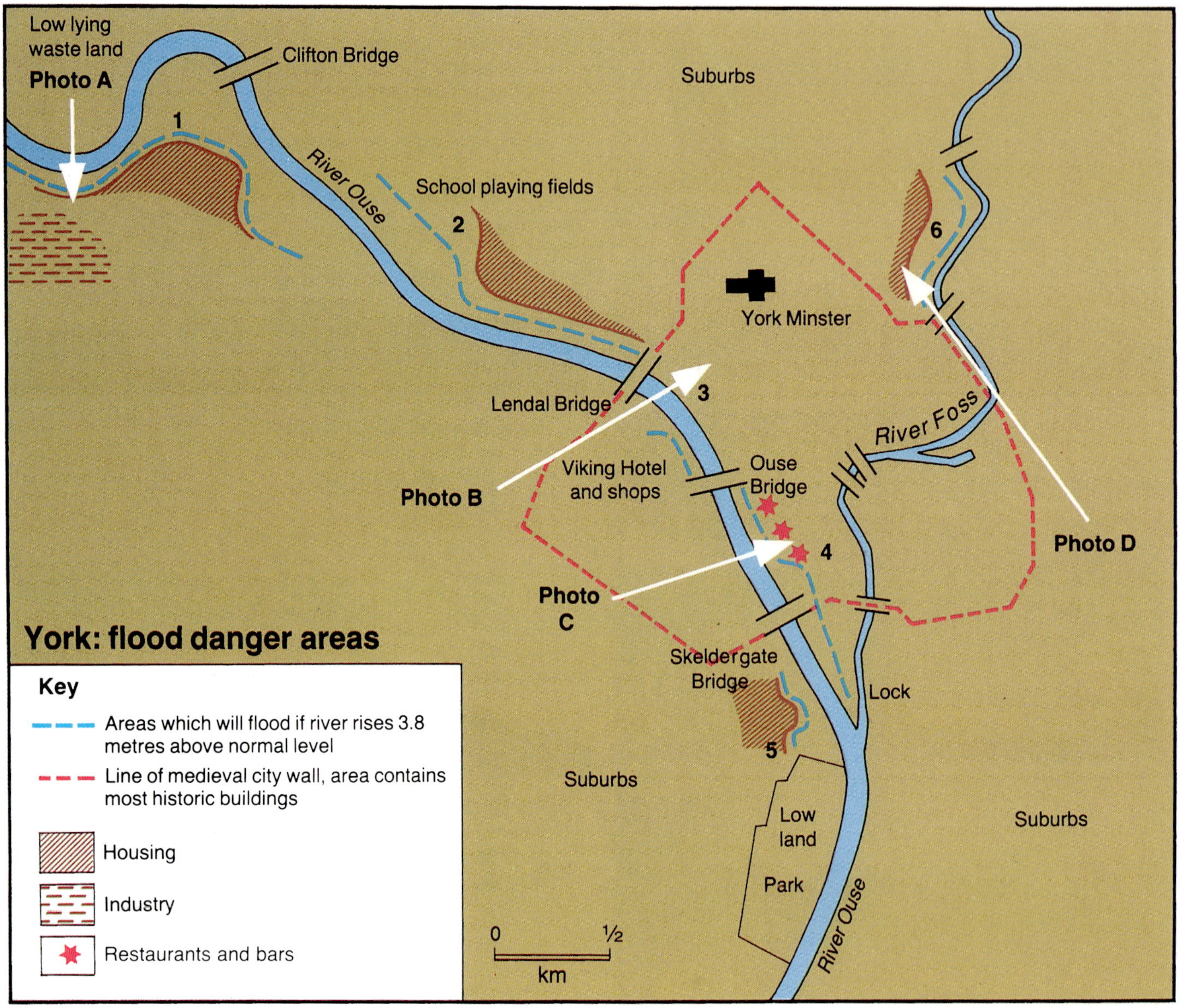

York: flood danger areas

Key
- — — Areas which will flood if river rises 3.8 metres above normal level
- — — Line of medieval city wall, area contains most historic buildings
- Housing
- Industry
- ★ Restaurants and bars

Map labels: Low lying waste land (Photo A), Clifton Bridge, Suburbs, River Ouse, School playing fields, York Minster, Lendal Bridge, Photo B, Viking Hotel and shops, Ouse Bridge, River Foss, Photo D, Photo C, Skeldergate Bridge, Lock, Suburbs, Low land Park, Suburbs.

The map shows the River Foss and the River Ouse and the land which is most at risk from floods. Look at the labels and the key. These tell you what the land is used for.

Study the map and the photographs. The positions where the photographs were taken are marked on the map.

Photo A

32

Photo B

Types of flood defence

Join with another person in the group and decide on the following:

1 What type of defence would be best to build on the course of the Ouse and Foss where these photographs were taken? Give at least one reason for your choice.

2 If there was only enough money to build three of the defences, which ones would you choose? Give reasons for your answer.

3 Are there any areas marked 1 – 6 on the map where building flood defences would spoil the environment? Give reasons for your answer.

4 Is there anywhere on the map that the Yorkshire Water Authority might use to drain water at the time of flood alert? Give reasons for your answer.

Photo C

Photo D

33

Unit 4

WEATHER

Rain or shine?

The weather is not the same in all parts of the country. If the weather is recorded for a whole year we notice large differences between places. It also varies from day to day. The weather from year to year in a region is known as the climate.

A climate graph is shown for Eastbourne. The figures are an average of temperature and rainfall figures over the last 50 years.

Eastbourne Climate graph

[Temperature graph showing °C from 0 to 25, months J F M A M J J A S O N D, with values approximately 4, 4, 6, 8, 11, 13, 15, 15, 14, 11, 8, 5]

[Rainfall graph showing mm from 0 to 250, months J F M A M J J A S O N D]

RANGE OF TEMPERATURE The difference between the highest and lowest monthly temperature

1 Look in your atlas and describe the LOCATION of:
(a) Eastbourne   (b) Keswick.

2 Use the climate graph of Eastbourne to give:
(a) the month with the highest temperature
(b) the highest temperature
(c) the month with the lowest temperature
(d) the lowest temperature
(e) the RANGE OF TEMPERATURE (take the lowest from the highest temperature)
(f) the total rainfall (add together the rainfall for each month).

3 (a) Use the climate figures for Keswick. Draw a climate graph like that for Eastbourne.
(b) Find the range of temperature for Keswick.
(c) Find the total rainfall for Keswick.

4 The climates of Keswick and Eastbourne are different. Join with a partner to make a list of all the differences you can find.

Keswick

34

Recording the weather

The weather forecast is worked out using information from:

(a) **Weather stations** – there are many weather stations in the British Isles which record all aspects of the weather. They send the information to the Meteorological Office each day.

(b) **Satellite** – the weather satellite sends pictures of the weather over large areas of Europe and the British Isles. These pictures can be picked up by the forecasters regularly through the day.

5 What is the difference between the weather information from the satellite and that from the weather stations on the ground?

6 Look at the picture of a weather station and the instruments used to record the weather.

(a) Why are the thermometers kept in the shade of the Stevenson Screen?

(b) Suggest why the sides of the Stevenson Screen have slits which allow the air into the screen.

7 Copy the drawing of the rain gauge. Put the following labels in the correct place.
Funnel – Grass to stop rain-drops bouncing – Collecting bottle – Copper tin – Ground.

A weather station

Temp (°C)		Rainfall (mm)
Jan	7	170
Feb	7	110
Mar	8	80
Apr	9	60
May	11	60
Jun	14	70
Jul	15	110
Aug	14	125
Sept	13	130
Oct	10	170
Nov	9	155
Dec	8	155

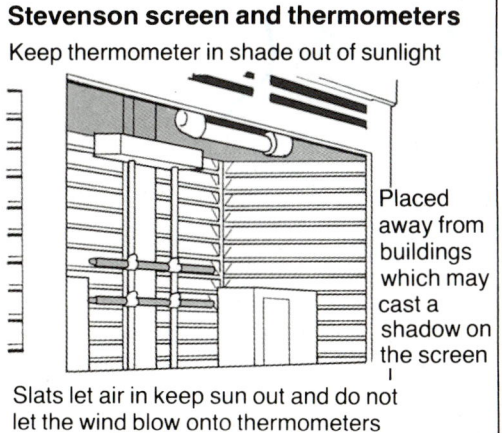

Stevenson screen and thermometers
Keep thermometer in shade out of sunlight
Placed away from buildings which may cast a shadow on the screen
Slats let air in keep sun out and do not let the wind blow onto thermometers

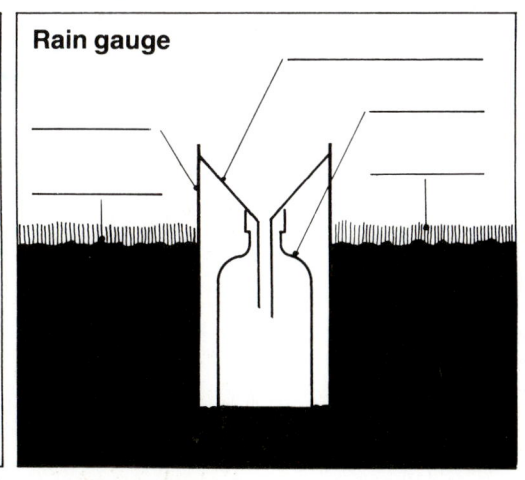

Rain gauge

Changeable weather

Look at the weather map.

"The weather in Eastern England is cool with westerly winds. A belt of rain lies across Scotland and England with another across Ireland. In Western England, Wales, and Southern Ireland the weather is warmer with westerly winds and scattered showers."

A FRONT
Marks the place where cold and warm air meet. In Britain they move from west to east. A warm front brings warm air behind it. A cold front brings cold air behind it

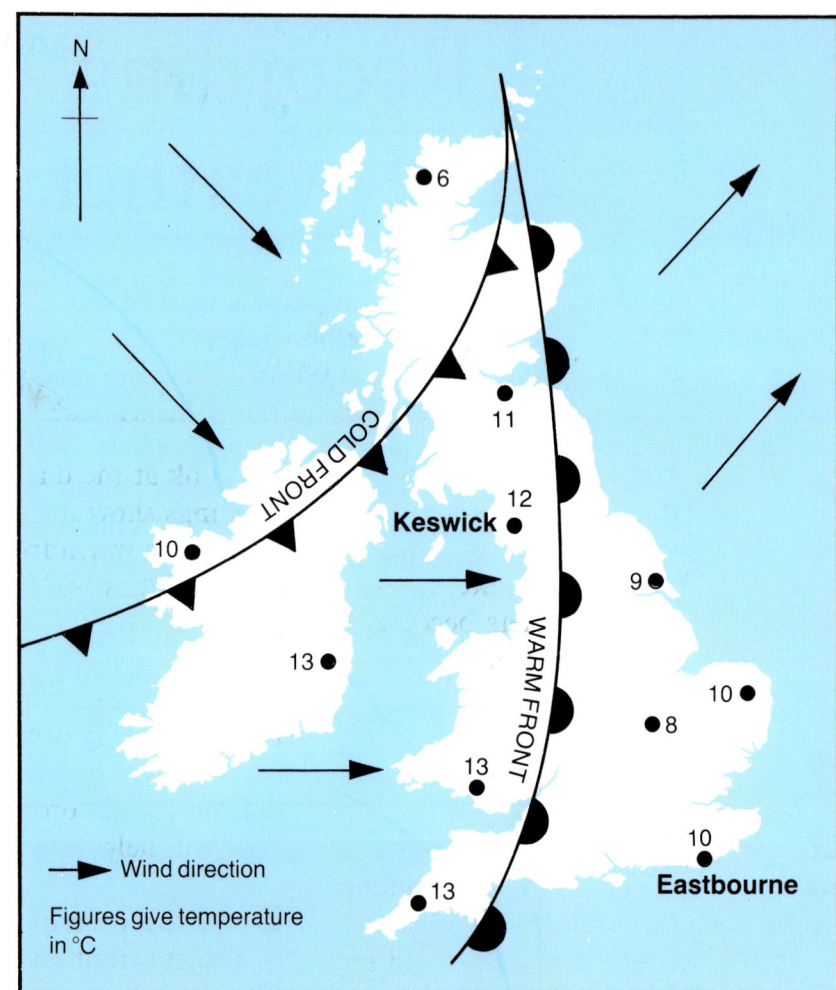

1 What are the temperatures at
(a) Eastbourne
(b) Keswick?

2 Draw the shape of the FRONTS like this.

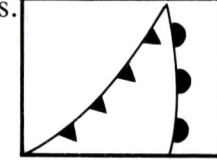

On your drawing:
(a) Shade (colour) warm air in red
(b) Shade cold air in blue.

3 Look at the following and write about the weather in Keswick:
(a) Find Keswick on the weather map
(b) Look at the weather for Keswick
(c) Read the weather forecast.

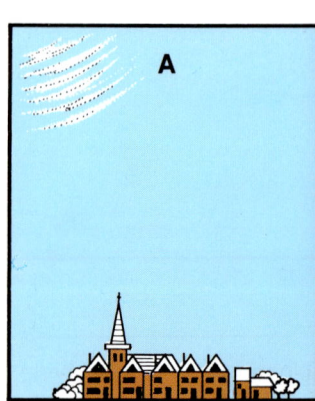

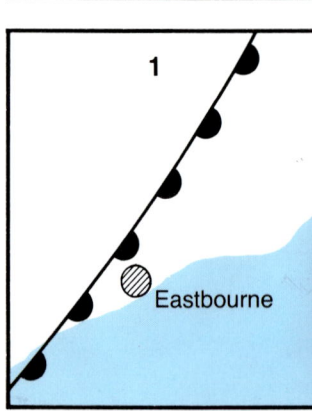

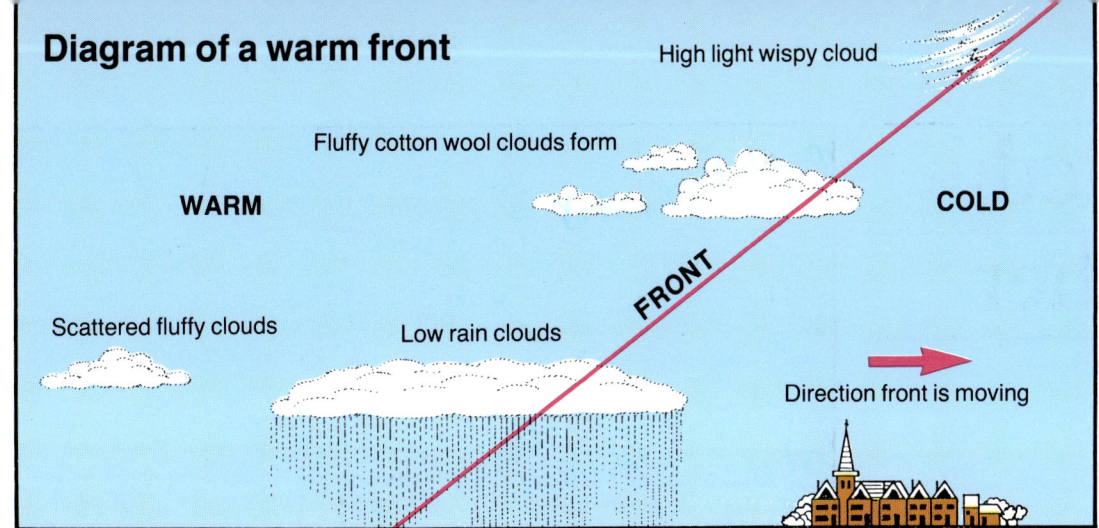

Warm air holds a lot of moisture. Warm air comes into contact with cold air. The moisture then forms droplets of water. The droplets make clouds. The air cools, the droplets become larger and they fall as rain.

4 Look at the diagram above of a warm front. Imagine you are standing in the town in the diagram. What would be the first sign you would see of a warm front approaching?

5 Look at the diagrams A–F. The drawings show the pattern of a warm front. The warm front is passing over a town. Draw and complete diagram B.

6 Look at the diagrams 1–6. A warm front is passing over Eastbourne. The drawings are in the wrong order. Write out the correct order. The diagrams A–F will help you.

7 Write a description of the weather as a warm front passes over Eastbourne.

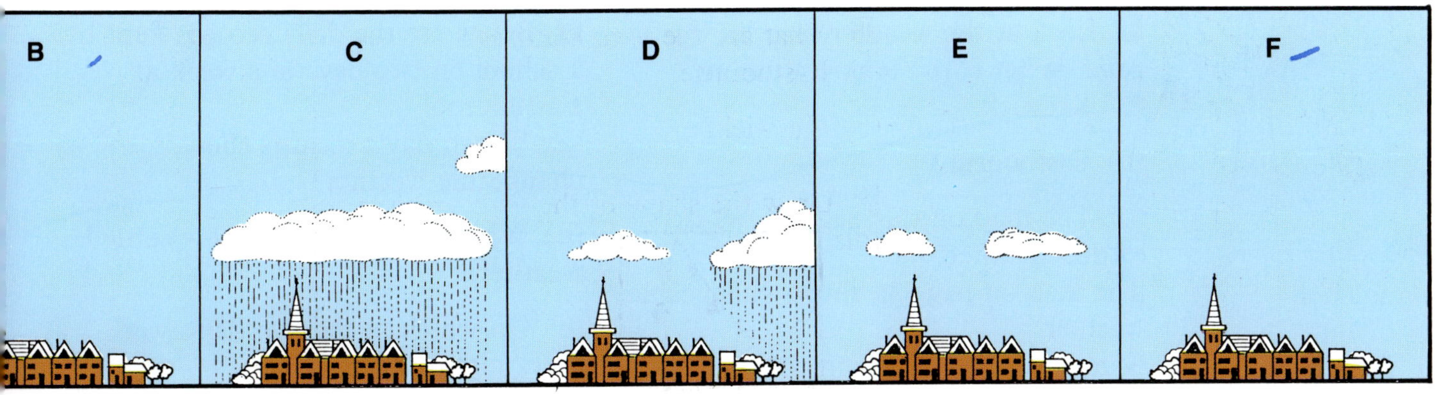

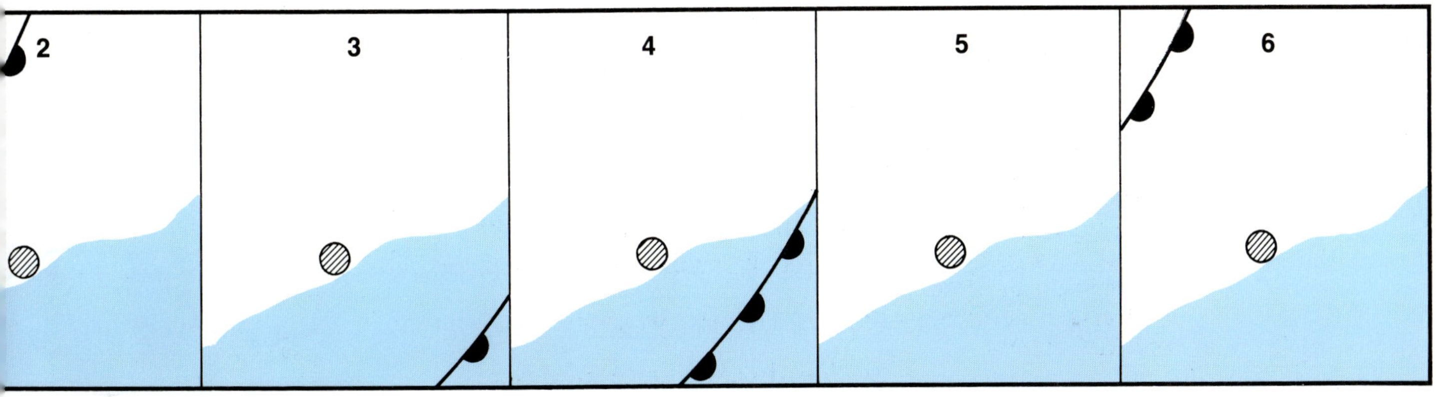

37

Settled weather

There is high pressure over the British Isles. We shall all have warm dry settled weather for the next few days. Winds will be light and there will be little cloud. There is a risk of thunderstorms breaking out later in the day.

Numbers give temperature in °C

1 Look at the weather map on this page. What is the temperature at:
(a) Keswick
(b) Eastbourne?

(c) The map on this page shows dry settled weather.
The map on page 36 shows changeable weather.
Give *three* ways in which they differ.

2 Below are the daily records kept by a school on two days in a week at Eastbourne.
(a) Which day's records show changeable weather?

(b) Which day's records show settled weather?

(c) On which of the two days was there high pressure?

(d) On which of the two days was the satellite photograph opposite taken – give full reasons for your answer.

	Windspeed (knots)	Wind direction	Temperature	Rainfall	Comment
Monday	15-18	WEST	8°C	6mm	SUNNY INTERVALS IN MORNING CLOUD AND RAIN IN AFTERNOON
Friday	0-1	NORTH	18°C	0	SUNSHINE ALL DAY NO CLOUD

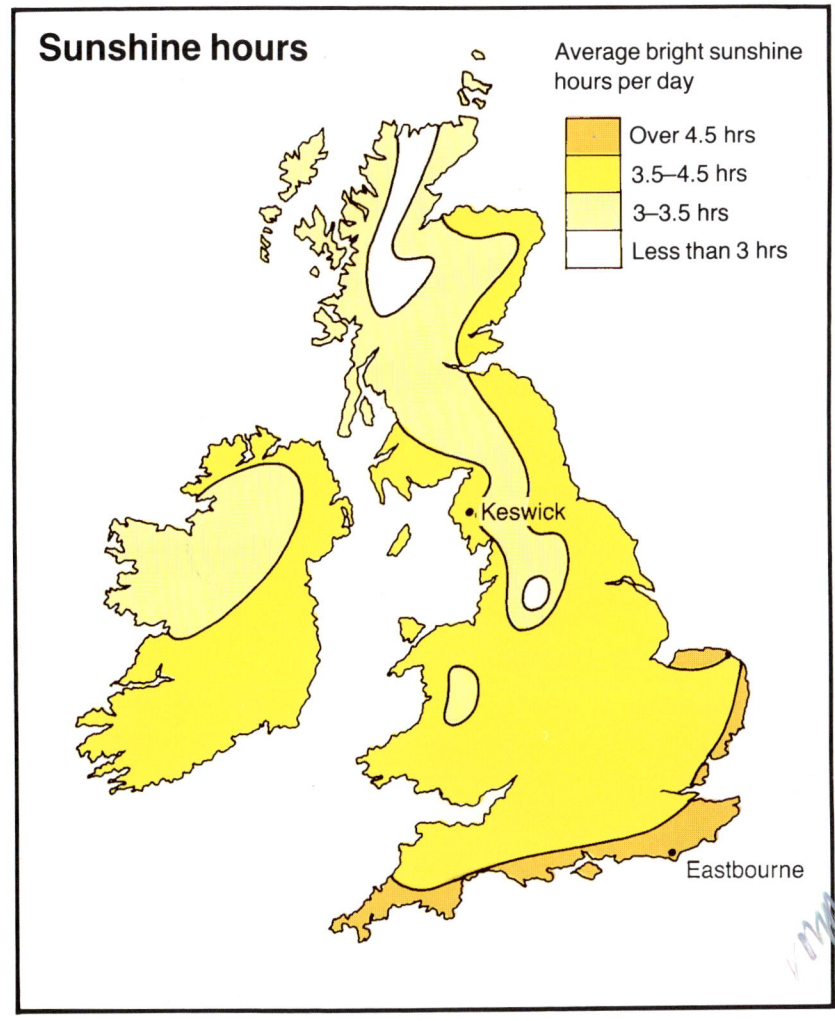

Sunshine hours

Average bright sunshine hours per day
- Over 4.5 hrs
- 3.5–4.5 hrs
- 3–3.5 hrs
- Less than 3 hrs

3 Look at the map showing the average length of daily sunshine in Great Britain.

(a) Where does the sun shine for over 4.5 hours?

(b) Where does the sun shine for under 3 hours?

(c) What is the average length of daily sunshine in
(i) Eastbourne   (ii) Keswick?

(d) Write three sentences about how hours of sunshine change from south to north in Britain.

The Sunshine Recorder

The sun shines through the glass ball which acts like a magnifying glass. There is a piece of paper behind the glass. The heat of the sun shines through the glass and burns a hole in the paper. As the sun moves round the sky a line is burnt in the paper. The line shows the hours of sunshine.

A sunshine recorder

Satellite photo of a depression over the British Isles

It all depends on the weather

1 (a) On a piece of tracing paper make a 10 × 10 grid of 1cm squares.

(b) Place your tracing paper over the map of 'British Isles – annual rainfall'. Put a cross in all the squares where the rainfall is over 1000mm per year.

(c) Place your tracing over the map of 'British Isles – relief'.
(i) How many squares with crosses in cover land over 250m?
(ii) How many squares without crosses cover land over 250m?

(d) From this information do you think there is a link between rainfall and height of land?

2 Write your own explanation of relief rainfall. Use the information on this page to help you.

3 Give one reason why Keswick has a higher annual rainfall than Eastbourne.

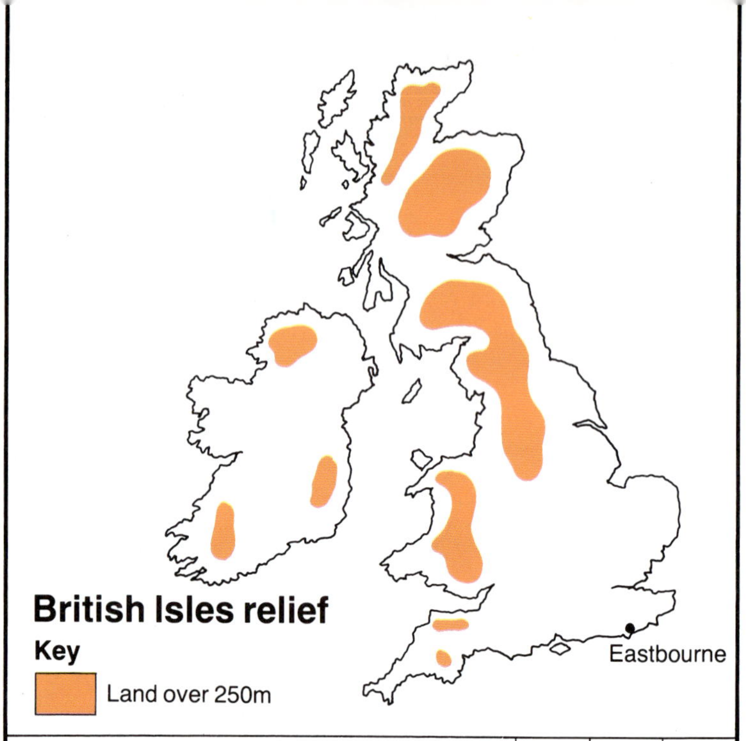

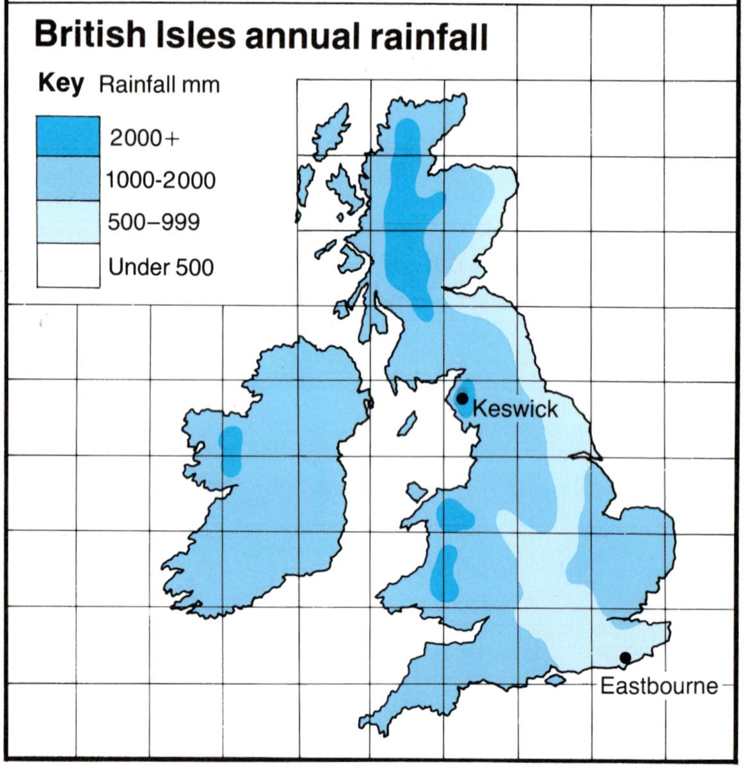

British Isles relief
Key
Land over 250m
Eastbourne

British Isles annual rainfall
Key Rainfall mm
2000+
1000-2000
500–999
Under 500
Keswick
Eastbourne

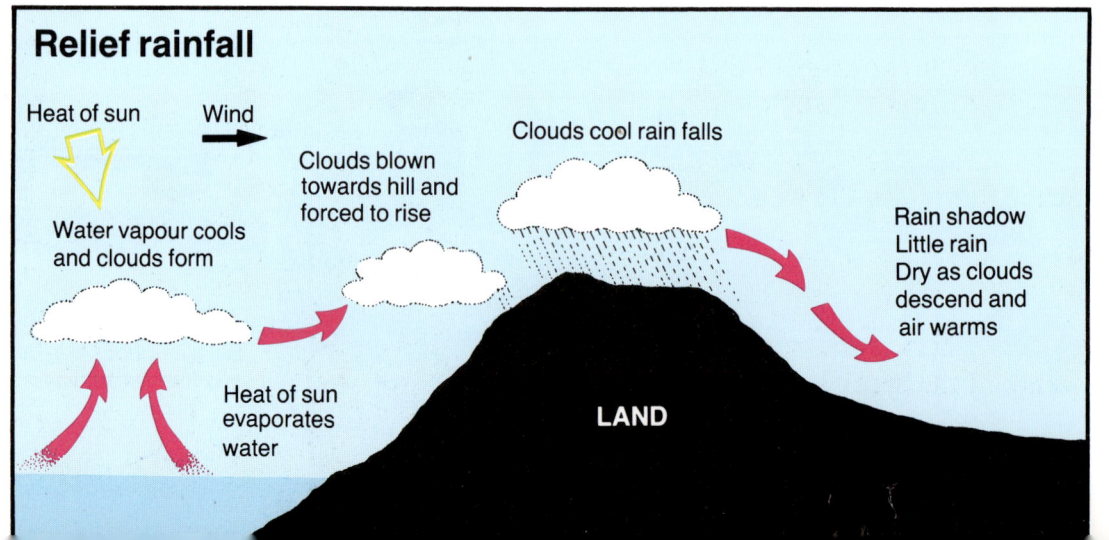

Relief rainfall
Heat of sun
Wind
Clouds cool rain falls
Clouds blown towards hill and forced to rise
Water vapour cools and clouds form
Rain shadow
Little rain
Dry as clouds descend and air warms
Heat of sun evaporates water
LAND

ANNUAL
Total over one year

RAIN SHADOW
Dry side of hills. It is the area shaded by hills from rainfall

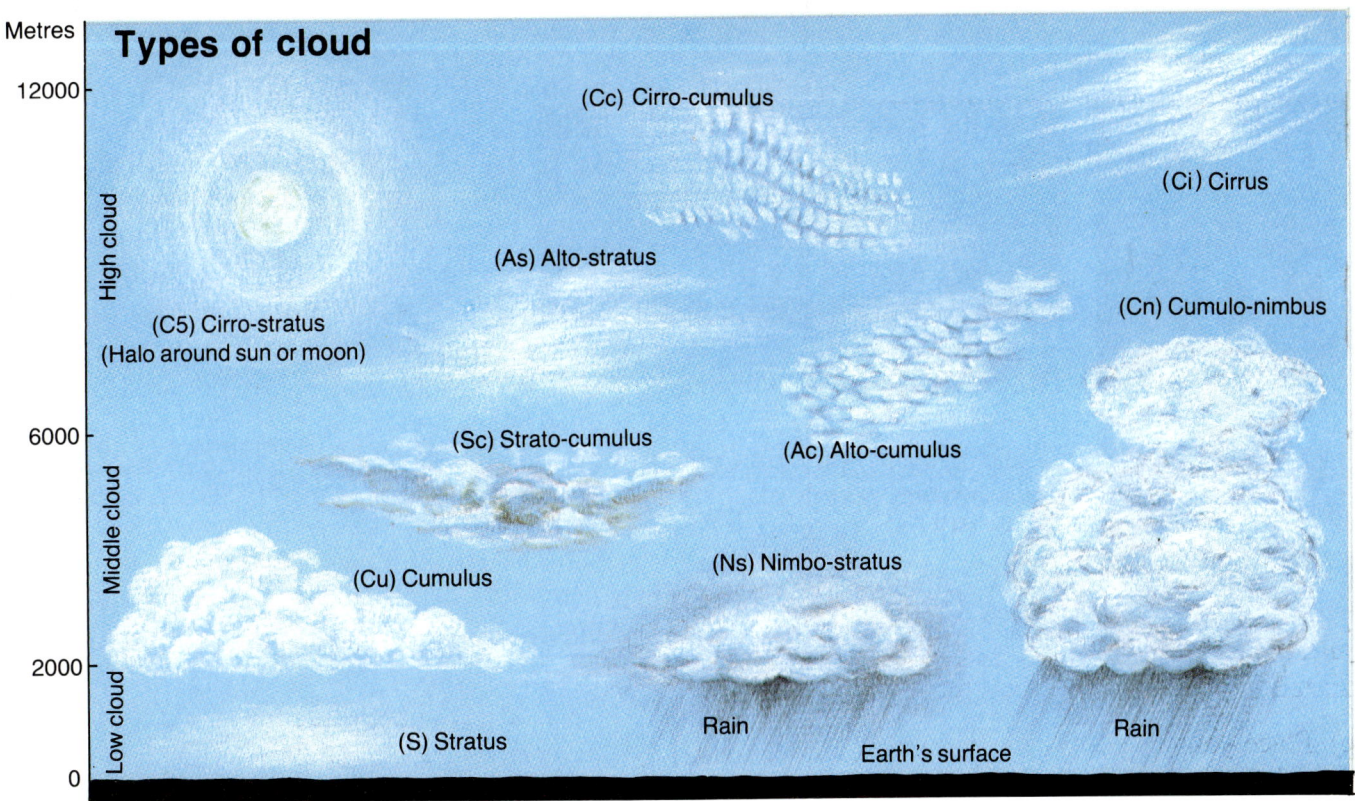

Types of cloud

(Cc) Cirro-cumulus
(Ci) Cirrus
(As) Alto-stratus
(Cn) Cumulo-nimbus
(C5) Cirro-stratus (Halo around sun or moon)
(Sc) Strato-cumulus
(Ac) Alto-cumulus
(Cu) Cumulus
(Ns) Nimbo-stratus
(S) Stratus

High cloud / Middle cloud / Low cloud

The amount of cloud in the sky is measured in eighths.
No cloud is $0/8$: A quarter of the sky covered is $2/8$: Half covered is $4/8$: Three quarters covered is $6/8$: Completely covered is $8/8$

4 Join with a group of friends. Set up a weather station. Prepare a chart like the one below, and keep a daily weather record on the chart. You will find information about measuring temperature, rainfall and wind on pages 15, 16, 35.

Here is a page from the weather record book. It shows readings taken from the school weather station by a group of students in Eastbourne.

5 Join with a friend and study the weather charts kept by the school in Eastbourne.
(a) In which week was the weather changeable?
(b) In which two days in that week did fronts cross the station?
(c) In which day in that week did a warm front cross the station?
(d) Why was the weather so calm and dry in the other week?
(e) What caused the rain on the Friday of the second week?

6 (a) Does Eastbourne or Keswick have the best weather for a holiday?
(b) Is weather the only thing to consider when you take a holiday?
(c) In which place Keswick or Eastbourne would you like to take a holiday?

Day	Temperature	Rainfall (mm)	Wind speed (knots)	Wind direction	Cloud	Cloud amount	Comment
Mon	14	2	10	SW	Ci	2/8	COOL CLEAR HIGH CLOUD
Tues	13	1	15	SW	NS	8/8	COOL WET am WARM pm
Wed	16	2	15	W	C	4/8	WARMER SCATTERED SHOWERS
Thur	16	2	18	W	C	4/8	MILD SCATTERED SHOWERS
Fri	13	8	16	NW	Cn	8/8	WET AND COOLER IN AFTERNOON
Sat	14	5	12	W	S	8/8	WET MORNING
Sun	17	0	8	N	C	7/8	WARM AND DRY
Mon	18	0	4	NE	AC	1/8	SLIGHT WIND DRY WARM
Tues	18	0	–	–	–	0/8	CLEAR AND WARM
Wed	20	0	–	–	–	0/8	DRY SUNNY ALL DAY
Thur	20	0	8	NE	Cn	0/8	SUNNY ALL DAY
Fri	18	0	–	–	–	3/8	RAIN IN AFTERNOON
Sat	20	0	–	–	–	0/8	SUNNY AN DRY
Sun	20	0	–	–	Ci	1/8	SUNNY AN WARM

Unit 5: Why coasts change

COASTS

The coastline is always changing. Are these changes caused by the sea and nature or by people? Can people stop these changes taking place?

The coastline we visit during the summer does not always stay the same. The description of the flood at Salthouse in 1978 and the two maps show that the coastline can change.

> Blakeney, where memories still lingered from the 1953 disaster, suffered some flooding leaving people trapped in upstairs rooms. Some boats were sunk, others were torn free and thrown up the streets, and in The Kings Head water reached a depth of 1.5 metres in the cellar. The next day it was 'business as usual', providing you were prepared to climb through the kitchen window to get your pint!
>
> The shingle ridge at Salthouse was breached in several places. 'The whole of the marsh and the coast road is flooded' reported the Anglian Water Board. 'We are stranded' reported the residents of Salthouse.

From an account of the flood of 1978 in *The Flooding of Eastern England* by M G and H J Harland

The probable growth of Blakeney Point

Map A Reconstruction of Blakeney Point [c. 1600 AD]

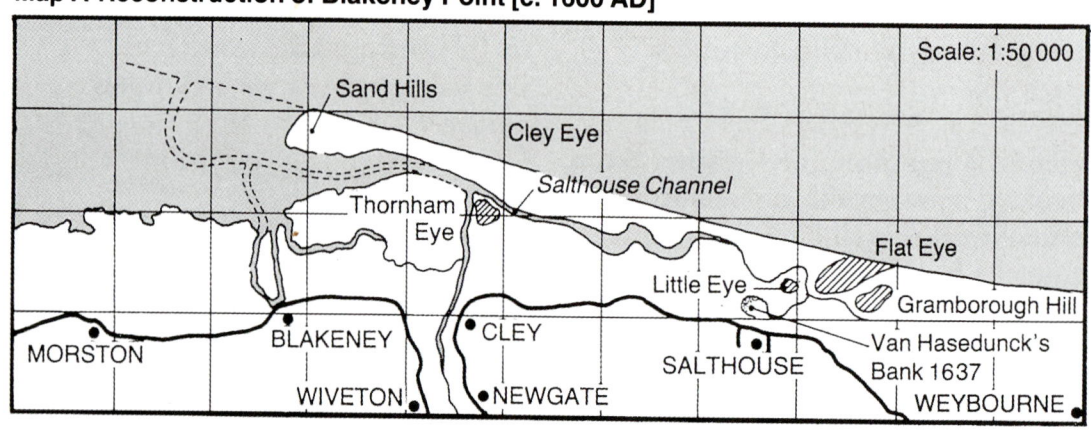

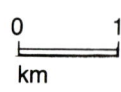

Map B Blakeney Point in 1988

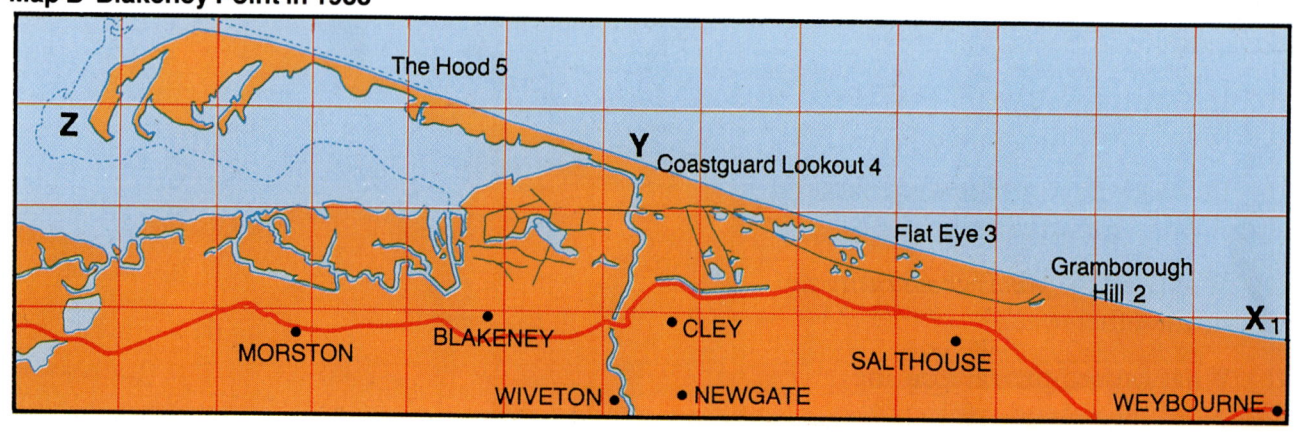

Photo 1

Photo 2

Photo 3

A flood will change the shape of the coast for a short time. The changes shown on the maps last much longer. They have taken place over many years.

1 Use the information on these pages to write one sentence to give clearly the location of Blakeney Point.

2 Use the maps of Blakeney Point to make a list of the changes in the coastline between 1600 (Map A) and 1988 (Map B).

3 Use Map B and its scale to write down how far the sea flooded from:
(a) the coast to Cley
(b) the coast to Salthouse.

4 Look at the photographs labelled 1, 2 and 3 on this page. They were taken at points X, Y and Z on Map B in 1988. Match the photograph with the correct letter and give one reason for your choice.

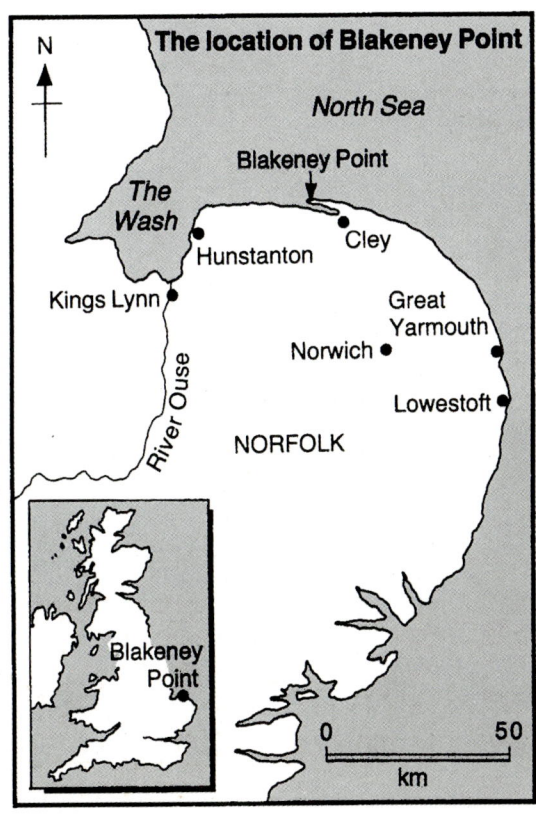

43

Sea cliffs

The sea cliffs are being worn away by the sea. Cliffs made of soft rock wear away easily. Cliffs made of hard rock take a long time to wear away. Cliffs made of hard and soft rock look different.

Nearly all the cliffs on the East coast are made of soft rock. This photograph shows what can happen when the cliffs are worn away. Many of the cliffs on the East coast of England are being worn away very quickly.

CORRASION
The cliff is worn away by small pieces of rock being smashed against it by the sea

---

HYDRAULIC ACTION
The cliff is weakened by air being pressed into cracks and then being sucked out by the sea

How the sea wears away the cliffs

The sea wears away the cliffs in two ways:

1 Small pieces of rock are smashed against the cliff by the sea this wears away the cliff. This is called CORRASION.

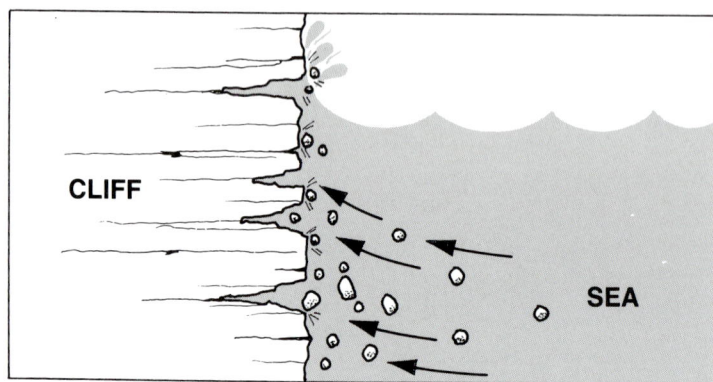

2 The sea pushes air into the cracks in the cliff. As the air rushes out of the crack the cliff is weakened. Pieces of cliff fall off. This is called HYDRAULIC ACTION.

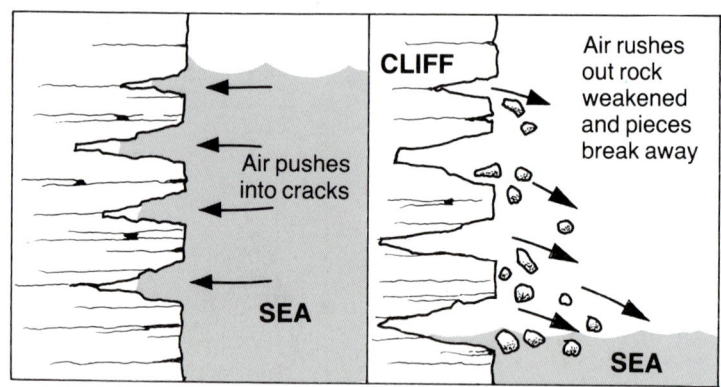

The small pieces of rock which break from the cliffs are knocked against each other. They break into small pieces.

Homes sometimes have to be abandoned after serious coastal erosion

This happens to cliffs made of soft rock

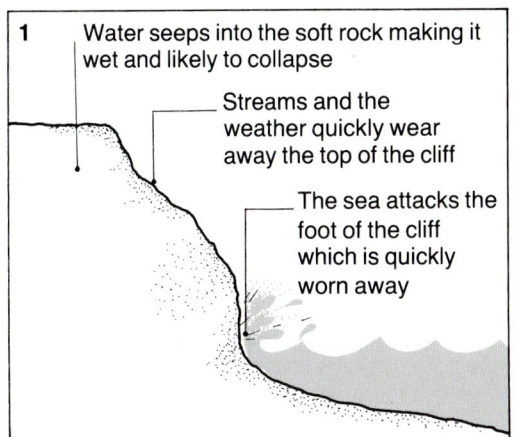
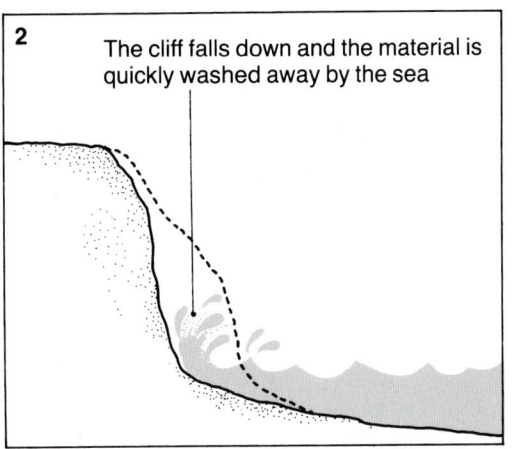

AN ARCH
An opening caused by the sea attacking a crack or weakness in the rock and wearing through a piece of land which juts out into the sea

A STACK
A piece of cliff left standing in the sea after an arch has fallen down or a cliff is worn away. It will slowly be worn away by the sea

This happens to cliffs made of hard rock

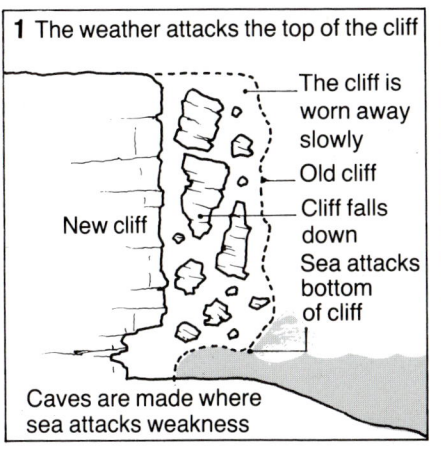
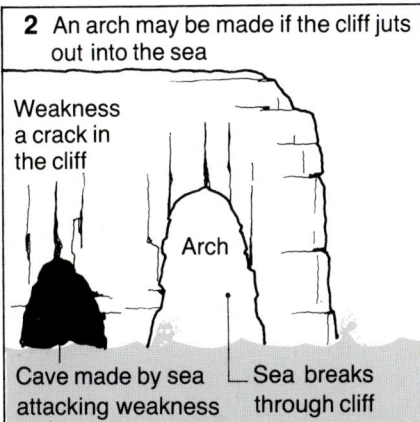
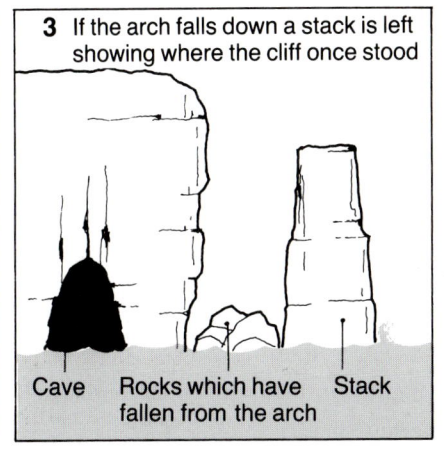

1 The sentences opposite are all about cliffs. Copy out the chart. Tick the box marked **Hard** if you think the sentence is about hard rock cliffs. Tick the box marked **Soft** if you think the sentence is about soft rock cliffs. Sometimes you will need to tick both boxes.

2 Make a list of the differences between cliffs made of hard rock and cliffs made of soft rock.
Your answers to question 1 and the diagrams on this page will help you.

3 Describe in your own words how a stack is made.

Sea Cliffs	Hard	Soft
Caves are found at the bottom of the cliff		
The cliff falls down and wears away quickly		
The sea attacks the bottom of the cliff		
The arch falls down		
The cliff is sloping rather than upright		
Stacks are found in the sea along the cliff		
It is unsafe to build houses near the edge of the cliff		
Large boulders are found at the bottom of the cliff		
The weather wears away the top of the cliff		
The sea quickly wears away the cliff material		

Shifting sands

Some of the material washed from the cliffs is moved along the coast by the sea.

1 Look at Experiment 1 carried out by Barton Manor School on the beach at Blakeney Point.
(a) What is the experiment trying to prove?
(b) What is the average distance the stones have moved?
(c) How many stones were found?
(d) Suggest what may have happened to the stones which were lost.
(e) Does the experiment prove what it was trying to prove?
(f) How could you improve on this experiment?

2 Look at Experiment 2 that was carried out on the same stretch of beach.
(a) Trace the pattern of canes shown.
(b) Join up the canes in number order.
(c) What pattern have you found?

Experiments 1 and 2 carried out by the students suggest that the sea moves sand and stones along the coast.

We know that the sea wears a great deal of material from the cliffs. Blakeney Point could be made of material which the sea has worn from the cliffs.

If this is true then the sea must have moved that material along the coast.

To discover whether the sea moves material along the coast at Blakeney Point

Experiment 1

This experiment was tried by students at Barton Manor School to see whether the sea moves material along the coast.

They placed coloured stones on the beach at low tide. They put a stick in the beach to show the position of the line (diagram 1).

The next day they looked at the stones at low tide. They plotted the position of as many coloured stones as they could find (diagram 2).

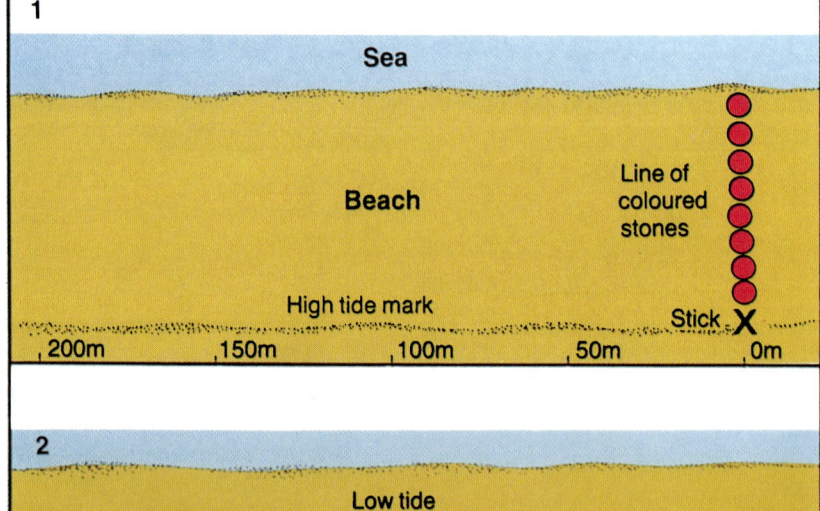

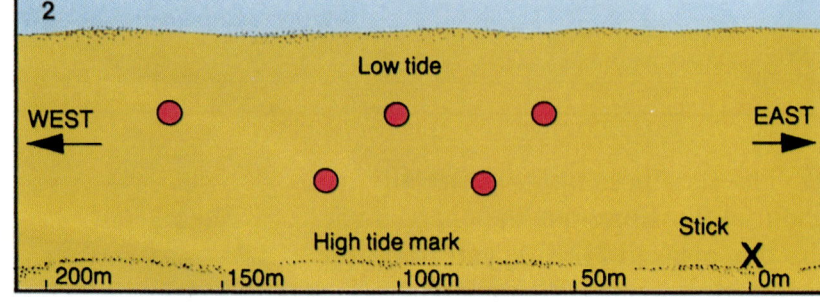

Experiment 2

The pupils of Barton Manor School floated a cork in the swash and backwash of the sea. They stuck long canes into the beach each time the cork changed direction.

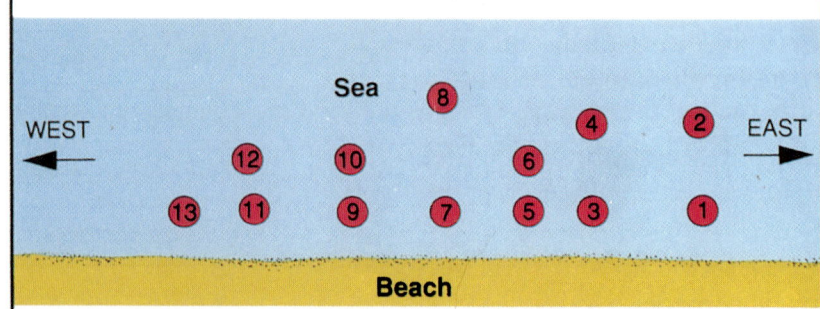

This is the pattern made by the canes at the end of the experiment at Blakeney Point.

SWASH
The rush of water up the beach after a wave breaks

BACKWASH
The water running back down the beach to the sea after the swash

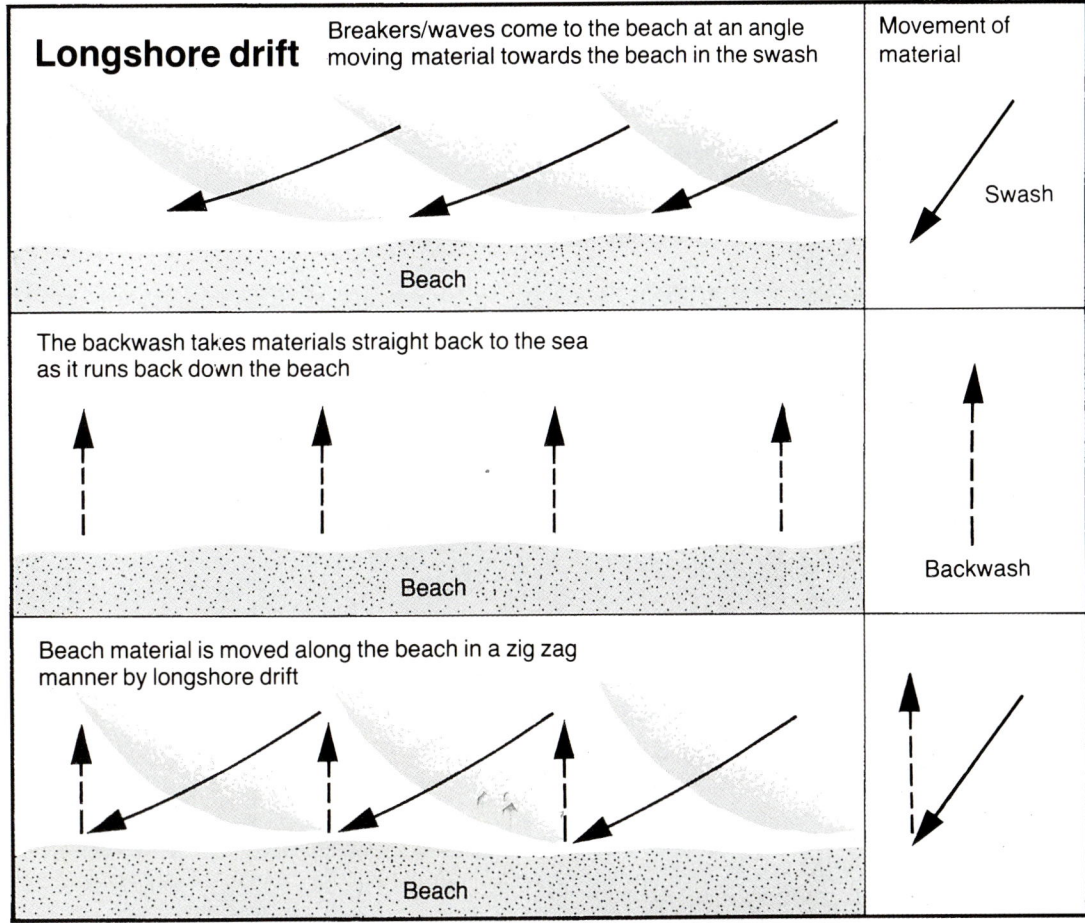

Look at the diagrams explaining longshore drift.

3 What is longshore drift?

4 How does longshore drift help to explain the pattern made by the canes?

5 Look at the data collected by the students in Experiment 3. What do you notice about the size of the pebbles?

6 Join with a friend and decide from the evidence on this page:
(a) whether the material is being moved along the beach at Blakeney and if so

(b) in which direction the material is being moved.
Give reasons for your decision.

(c) What happens to the size of the pebbles at Blakeney Point as you move further away from the cliff at Weybourne?

(d) Suggest reasons why the size of pebbles changes.

Experiment 3

The pupils also measured the size of the pebbles at five places on Blakeney Point. these are shown on the map as numbers 1–5. At each place the students measured a sample of 50 pebbles. Here are the results.

Mean size (diameter) of all pebbles measured at				
The Hood 5	Cley 4	Flat Eye 3	Gramborough Hill 2	Weybourne 1
18.4mm	24.6mm	26.2mm	27.9mm	29.7mm

The making of Blakeney Point....

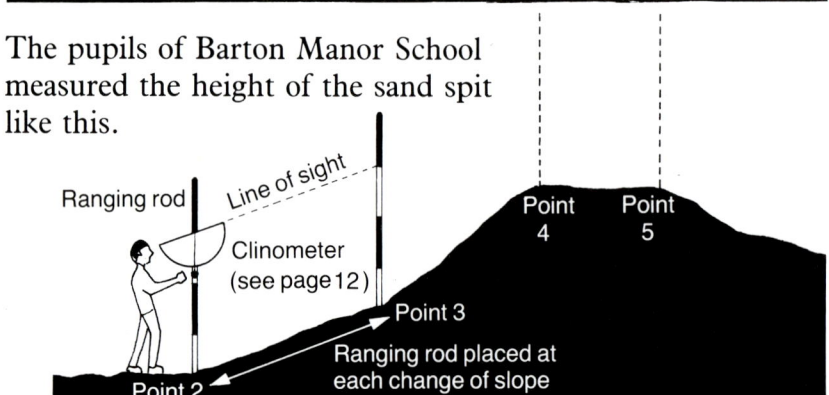

Features of coastal deposition

Streams will bring freshwater to this lagoon. They will also bring silt which will eventually fill the lagoon. Plants will grow and new land forms.

How does longshore drift make a formation like Blakeney Point?

The material is brought along the coast by longshore drift. It reaches the end of Blakeney Point. Then it has no more coast to move along so the material is deposited.

A feature like Blakeney Point is called a SAND SPIT.

1 Look at the map of Blakeney Point in 1600 AD and 1988.
How far has Blakeney Point grown in the 385 years between the two dates?

The pupils of Barton Manor School measured the height of the sand spit like this.

Point to point		Distance (metres)	Height (cm)
1 (sea level)	2	50	+100
2	3	10	+50
3	4	10	+150
4	5	20	0
5	6	15	-200
6	7	15	-50
7 (marsh)	8	30	-40

2 Describe how the measurements were taken. Use the diagram above and the information on measuring slopes on page 12.

3 Use graph paper to draw a diagram of the results like the one below. The first three have been plotted for you.

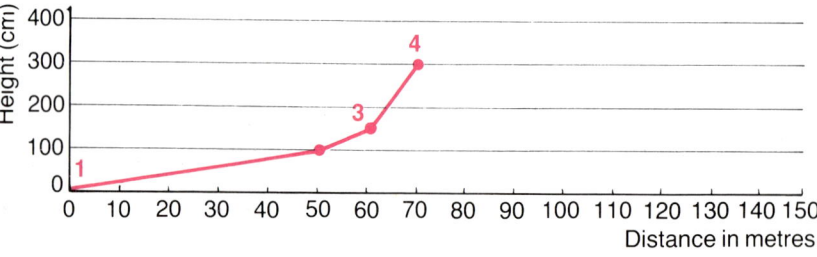

SAND SPIT
A long narrow piece of land jutting out into the sea formed from sand and shingle washed along the coast

....and the marshland

The marshland at Blakeney Point

A variety of plants gradually begins to grow on the spit and the land behind it. Once they become established SILT collects round them.

The water makes deep gullies or CREEKS around the plants and a salt marsh is formed. The sea seeps into this MARSH and only the specially adapted salt marsh plants are able to survive. Other plants would be killed by the salt.

4 What is a salt marsh?

5 Explain to your partner how a salt marsh is formed. Ask two questions to see if you have been understood.

6 Three salt marsh plants are shown here. Other plants growing in salt marshes are Eel Grass, Marsh Samphire, Sea Lavender, Sea Pinks, Sea Aster and Red Fescue. Try to find a picture of two of these and draw them.

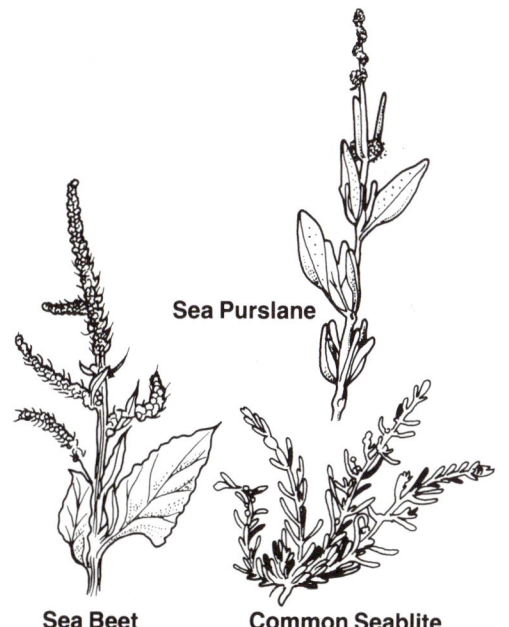

Sea Purslane

Sea Beet   Common Seablite

SILT
Fine sandy material like mud carried by the sea, and deposited in calm water

CREEK
A long narrow twisting tidal inlet of the sea, found in marshy areas of the coast

MARSH
A large very wet area of land which at the coast is often known as salt marsh. This area contains many plants able to survive in the salty sea water conditions

Formation of a salt marsh

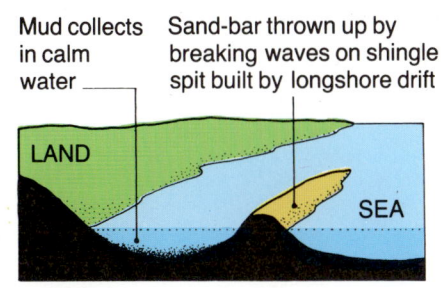

Mud collects in calm water — Sand-bar thrown up by breaking waves on shingle spit built by longshore drift

Salt-water plants begin to grow in the mud. Their leaves and roots trap even more mud on which further plants grow — Sand-bar or shingle spit

Pools of salt-water trapped to form salt-pans — Winding creeks draining marsh to sea — Protecting bar or spit

People and coasts

People often attempt to stop coasts changing.

The bulldozer in the photograph below is building up Blakeney Point at Cley. It is pushing the shingle into a higher ridge. People hope that the high ridge will protect the land behind it from flooding.

Where there are cliffs people use other methods of protecting the bottom of the cliff from the pounding of the sea.

1 Look at the map.
(a) What is the area between Cley and the sea used for?

(b) Do you think this area is worth protecting with an expensive sea wall? Give a reason for your answer.

2 People think that bulldozing the shingle at Blakeney Point is better than building a sea wall.
(a) Why do you think bulldozing is thought to be better than building a sea wall?

(b) What is the disadvantage of this method of protecting the land?

3 Give one reason why we should protect cliffs from the sea.

4 Give one reason why we should not protect cliffs from the sea.

5 Which of the two types of cliff – those made of hard or soft rock – are most in need of protection? Give a reason for your answer.

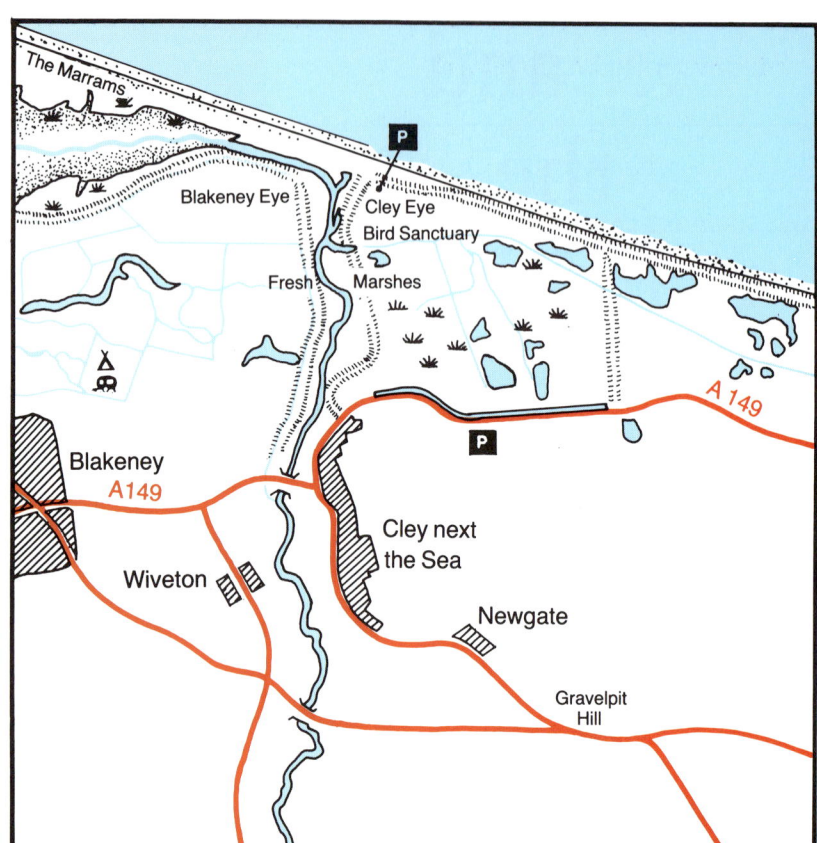

Sea wall or shinglebank?

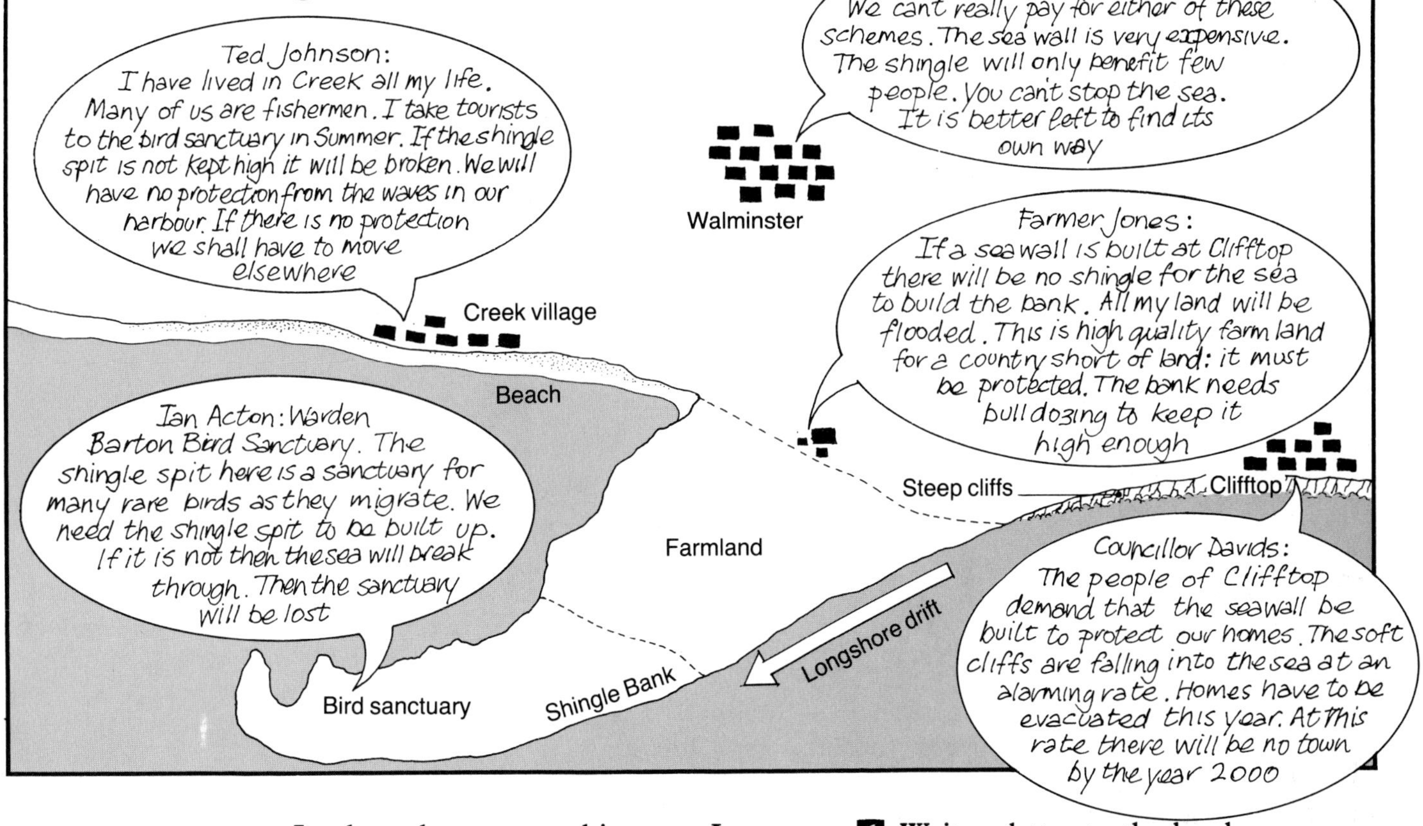

Ted Johnson: I have lived in Creek all my life. Many of us are fishermen. I take tourists to the bird sanctuary in Summer. If the shingle spit is not kept high it will be broken. We will have no protection from the waves in our harbour. If there is no protection we shall have to move elsewhere

Harold Jackson: County Councillor We can't really pay for either of these schemes. The sea wall is very expensive. The shingle will only benefit few people. You can't stop the sea. It is better left to find its own way

Farmer Jones: If a sea wall is built at Clifftop there will be no shingle for the sea to build the bank. All my land will be flooded. This is high quality farm land for a country short of land: it must be protected. The bank needs bulldozing to keep it high enough

Ian Acton: Warden Barton Bird Sanctuary. The shingle spit here is a sanctuary for many rare birds as they migrate. We need the shingle spit to be built up. If it is not then the sea will break through. Then the sanctuary will be lost

Councillor Davids: The people of Clifftop demand that the sea wall be built to protect our homes. The soft cliffs are falling into the sea at an alarming rate. Homes have to be evacuated this year. At this rate there will be no town by the year 2000

Map labels: Walminster, Creek village, Beach, Farmland, Steep cliffs, Clifftop, Shingle Bank, Bird sanctuary, Longshore drift

Here in Norfolk (left), an attempt has been made to protect the crumbling cliffs with groynes and huge wooden wave-breakers

A bulldozer raising the shingle bank (below)

Look at the map on this page. It shows a piece of coastline at Walminster. The people have a choice of plans to protect the land.

Plan 1 – They could build a sea wall at Cliff-top. The sea wall would protect the town from the cliffs crumbling away.

Plan 2 – They could make the shingle spit higher. A higher shingle spit would stop the sea flooding in and the spit being washed away.

6 Write a letter to the local Walminster Gazette. Imagine it is sent from one of the people who speak on the map. Set out their point of view about the sea wall or the shingle bank.

7 What solution to the problem do you favour?

8 Join with others who have the same point of view as your own. Find as many reasons as you can to support your view.

9 A march to Walminster County Hall is planned. The people plan to tell the councillors how they feel. Design a placard that you could hold on the march.

10 The County Council has called a meeting. They want everyone's ideas about the sea wall and shingle bank. Discuss with others in your class the reasons for your group's view.

Unit 6
VOLCANOES

The power of the earth
Where are volcanoes?

Every year volcanoes ERUPT in different parts of the world. We hear about these on television news. Some eruptions can cause loss of life on a large scale. The Nevada del Ruiz volcano erupted on a large scale in Colombia, South America in November 1985. Approximately 20 000 people were killed by the mudflows which spread through towns and villages on the lower slopes of the volcano. Other volcanoes might erupt and damage the environment very seriously. Mount St Helens in the north west of the USA erupted in May 1980. The eruption damaged forests and destroyed wildlife. The landscape was covered in dust for thousands of square kilometres.

1 Using an atlas to help you, find out which country the following volcanoes are in:
(a) Mauna Loa (b) Vesuvius
(c) Fujiyama (d) Popocatepetl.

2 Write a short paragraph to describe why volcanoes are dangerous.
(Useful words: explode, erupt, noise, lava.)

The earth is made up of different layers of material. These layers are shown in the diagram opposite.

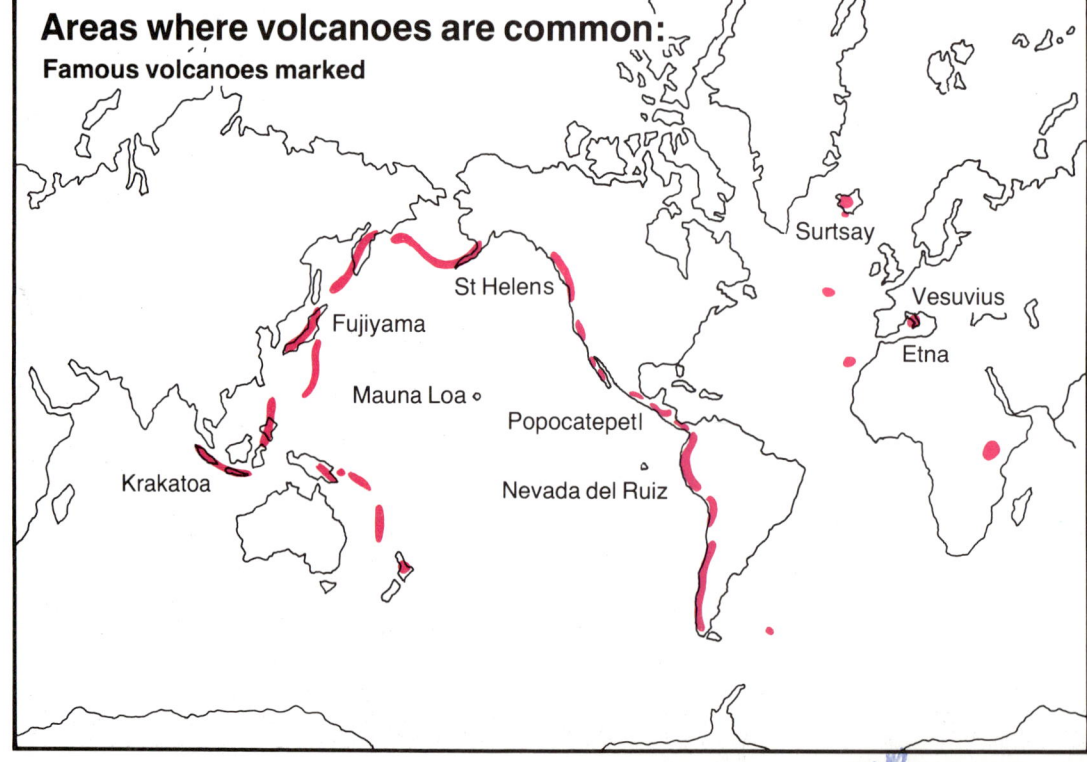

Areas where volcanoes are common:
Famous volcanoes marked

52

Etna erupting: a spectacular firework display

The crust is divided up into a number of sections. We call these PLATES. The plates are very large. Sometimes they are as big as the whole of a CONTINENT. The map on this page shows the plates which make up the earth's crust.

The plates do not stand still. They move very slowly. They can move away from one another or together. The places where the plates join are very unstable parts of the earth's crust.

The outer layer of the earth is made of solid rock about 30km thick. The rock is known as the crust. The crust is thin when compared with the total depth of the earth from surface to core.

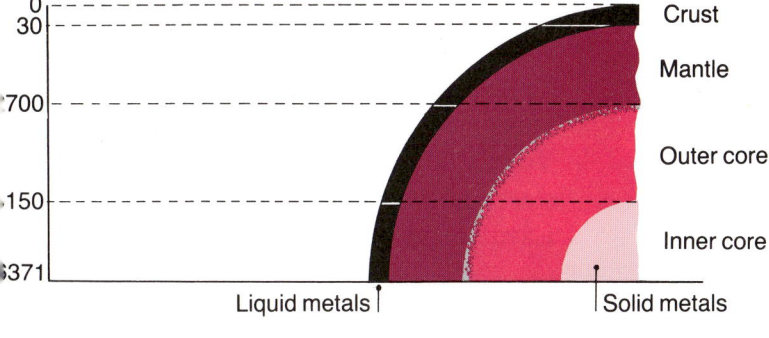

3 Trace the map 'Areas where volcanoes are common'.

4 Place the tracing over the map below. Notice the position of the volcanoes and where the plates join. Write a sentence about what you notice.

5 Using the information on this page, write a description of the earth's surface and how it is made up.

At the position on the earth's surface where plates join, volcanoes, earthquakes and mountains are often found. These areas can be the most dangerous places on the earth.

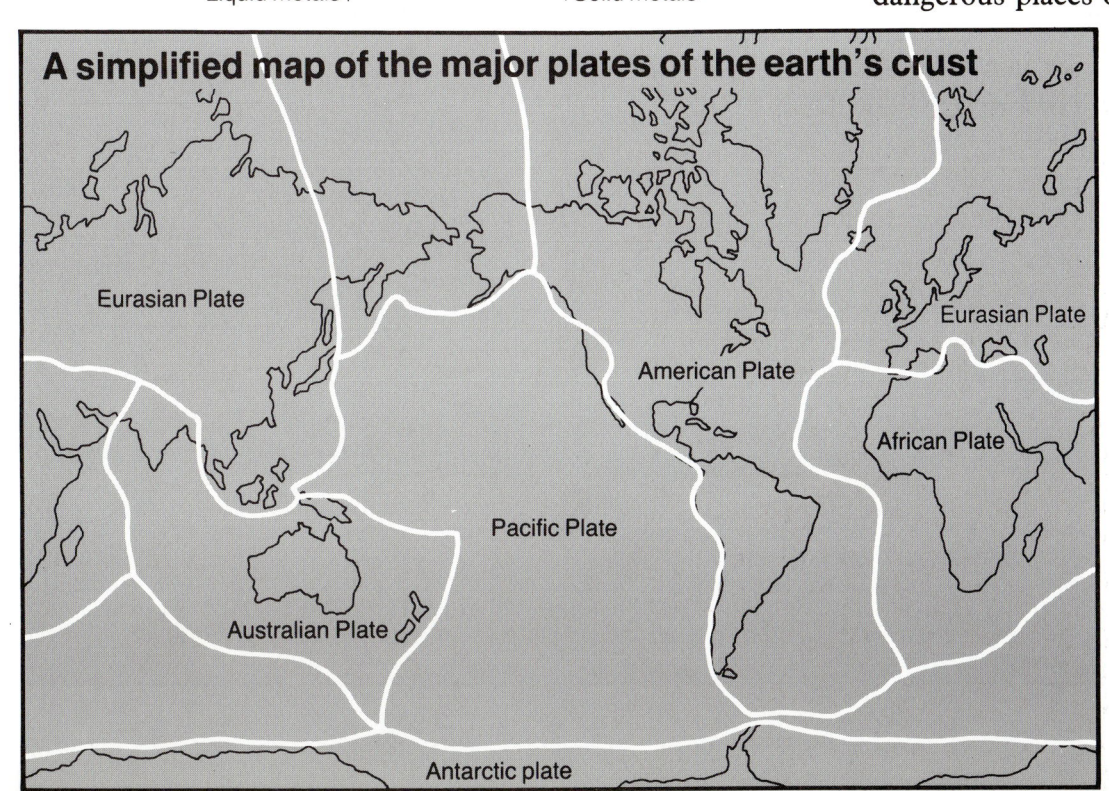

ERUPT
When a volcano pours out hot lava

PLATE
A huge section of the earth's crust which could be land surface or could extend under the sea

CONTINENT
A large land mass which contains a number of countries

How do volcanoes erupt?

Plates moving towards each other COLLIDE. The way in which they collide is shown in the diagram below. Two things happen.
1 One plate bends under the other.
2 One plate crashes into the other. Then surface rocks begin to fold together to form FOLD MOUNTAINS.

When great masses of rock collide there is a great deal of FRICTION where they crash.

Where one plate bends under the other, friction and pressure cause intense heat. In this area of intense heat solid material can sometimes melt. Some of the molten rock may force itself into the earth's surface layers. It may reach the earth's surface. The molten rock will move along a line of weakness in the earth's surface layers. Sometimes the molten rock is stored in a MAGMA chamber.

Pressure builds up in the chamber. Then the molten rock forces its way along a crack to the surface. When it appears at the surface it is called LAVA. Gradually the lava flows out of the crack, cools and turns into solid rock. The crack is called a VENT.

Quite often steam, ash and dust pour out of the vent before the lava. The ash and dust settle on the last lava flow. A volcanic cone is formed.

1 Copy the diagram of the volcanic cone. Label the vent, layers of ash and lava and the magma chamber.

2 Add details of the following events. Place the comments in the correct boxes.
– Lava flows down the side of the cone.
– Volcano explodes throwing out ash, steam and dust.
– Lava spills out of the cone.

COLLIDE
Crash together

FOLD MOUNTAINS
Mountains which form when plates collide, surface rocks become folded

FRICTION
The rubbing together of two surfaces often causing heat energy

LAVA
Molten rock in contact with air

MAGMA
Molten rock inside the earth's crust

VENT
The point where lava flows out

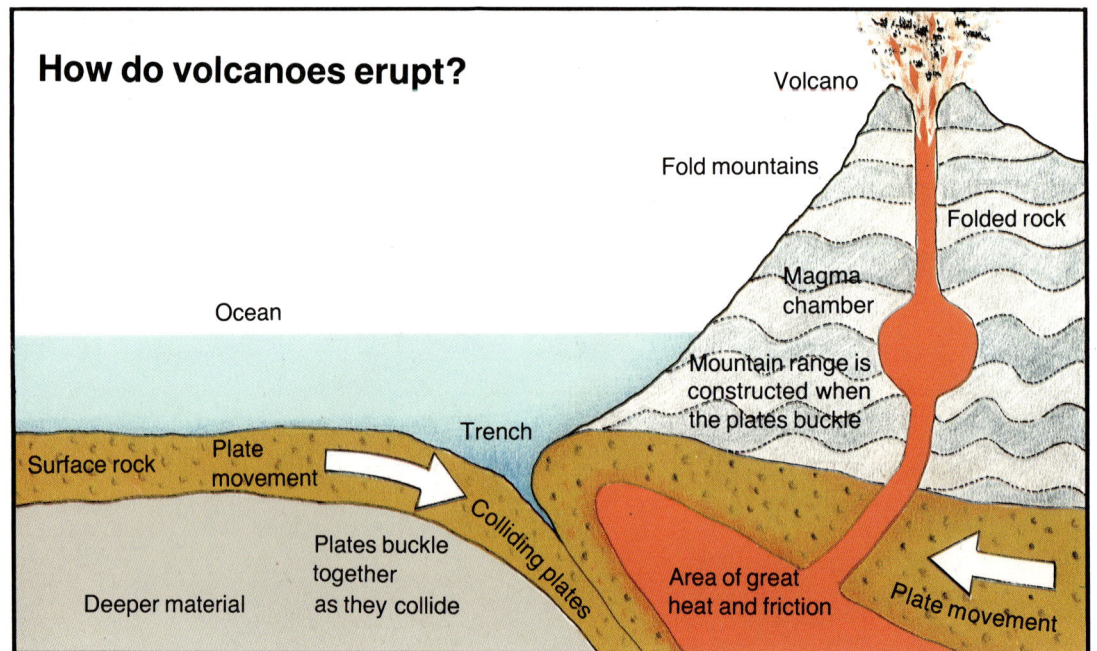

Etna exploding smoke, steam and ash (top left)
Etna exploding lumps of red hot lava (top right)
Etna: lava flows (bottom left)
Etna: dormant but steaming (bottom right)

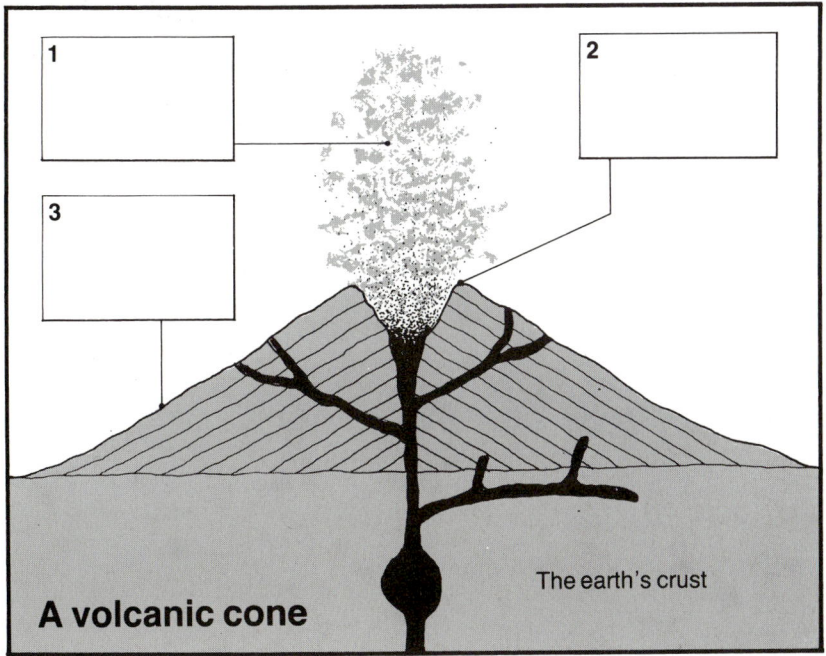

A volcanic cone

The earth's crust

55

Etna: an active volcano

Etna is one of the largest volcanoes on earth and is the biggest in Europe. The peak is 3340 metres above sea level. It is 300 km round the base. Etna is an active volcano which constantly rumbles and steams. When it erupts it looks like an exciting firework display. However, it can badly damage land and property.

Living close to the volcano is a danger. Villagers and farmers who live on the slopes of Etna are afraid of what might happen. The people always say that they are worried when Etna suddenly goes quiet.

The lava can be red-hot when it forces its way out of the vent. The lava then runs down the mountain. It spreads to the valleys around Etna. The longer the eruption lasts the more destruction is caused. It does not matter how wide the vent is. The worst eruptions are those which have lasted for months or years.

Etna destroying crops (left)

Lava destroying buildings on the slopes of Etna (below)

1 Describe the location of Mount Etna.

2 What is meant by the term 'an active volcano'?

3 Copy and complete the following paragraph by filling in the missing words. Use the information on the page opposite.

The lava when it flows out of the vent is ____ ____. The amount of destruction the lava causes depends on the length of ____ over which the eruption takes place, not the ____ of the ____.

4 Join with a friend. You are two reporters working for a newspaper. You have flown out to Palermo, the capital of Sicily, to cover the latest eruption of Etna. Your job is to write a front page newspaper report and to draw an exciting picture.

Your report should tell your readers:

(a) How long the eruption has been happening.

(b) How fast the lava is flowing.

(c) How hot the lava is.

(d) How close you can get to the lava before it becomes uncomfortable.

(e) How much damage is being caused.

(f) If the authorities are thinking about evacuating people.

(g) If any roads have been blocked or telephone lines broken.

How do we stop a lava flow?

An emergency team meet to think about the problem of the volcano. They have to decide what action to take. You are in the team. Join with the others to decide how to deal with the situation.

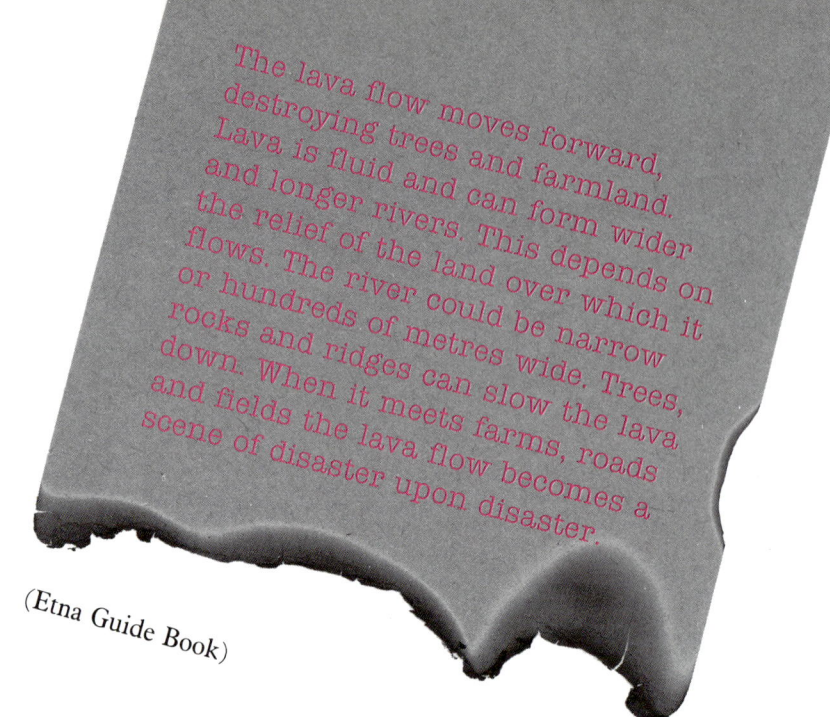

The lava flow moves forward, destroying trees and farmland. Lava is fluid and can form wider and longer rivers. This depends on the relief of the land over which it flows. The river could be narrow or hundreds of metres wide. Trees, rocks and ridges can slow the lava down. When it meets farms, roads and fields the lava flow becomes a scene of disaster upon disaster.

(Etna Guide Book)

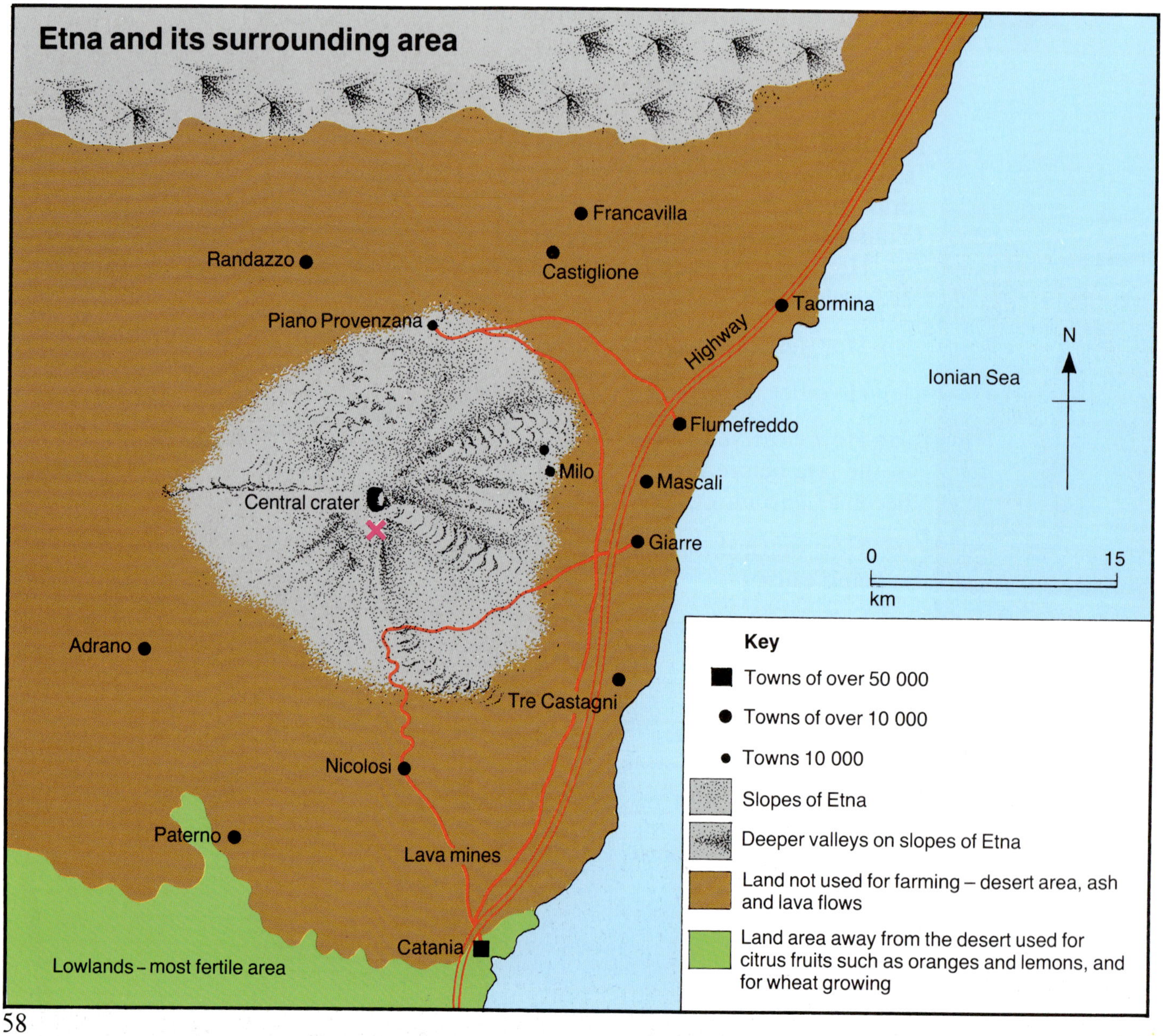

Etna and its surrounding area

Key
- ■ Towns of over 50 000
- ● Towns of over 10 000
- • Towns 10 000
- Slopes of Etna
- Deeper valleys on slopes of Etna
- Land not used for farming – desert area, ash and lava flows
- Land area away from the desert used for citrus fruits such as oranges and lemons, and for wheat growing

The town of Nicolosi is to the south of the main crater. The lava flow is heading for Nicolosi. The emergency team have to stop the lava flow from reaching the town. The volcano has been erupting for two weeks. There seems to be no chance of the flow ending.

A team of engineers have thought of a way of stopping the lava flow. The lava is coming from a new vent. The vent is close to the central crater (marked X on the map). The engineers think that they can change the direction of the flow. They want to place explosives close to the new vent. The lava will then flow to the north, east or west.

1 (a) Which towns and villages need evacuating first?

(b) What types of vehicle are needed?

(c) What should people being evacuated take with them?

(d) Where are you going to take the evacuated people?

2 Your team have to decide which way to divert the lava.
Consider the following:
(a) Number and size of towns and villages on the lava path.

(b) Valleys where lava could collect.

(c) Wider areas of land for the lava to spread harmlessly.

(d) Farmland in danger. Roads which may be blocked.

Give at least three reasons for your decision.

Devastation on the slopes of Etna

Unit 7

LOWLANDS

Changing environments

The marshlands of East Norfolk

Halvergate Marshes are an example of what lowlands were like in many parts of Eastern England.

Large areas of East Norfolk can be described as marshland. These areas are used for grazing cattle in the summer months. The land is very low; the height is near to or sometimes below sea level. Over 300 years ago the marshlands were very wet and muddy and were often flooded at high tide. In the 17th Century wind-pumps, drainage ditches and SLUICES were built to help drain the land and make it possible for farmers to use. Today the wind-pumps are no longer used.

The photograph opposite shows a view of a marshland environment in Norfolk. These environments have the following features:

1. Wide open views, sometimes broken by clumps of trees.
2. DYKES with thick, rich vegetation at their edges.
3. Colourful landscapes.
4. Grazing animals.
5. Wildlife (particularly birdlife).
6. Wind-pumps.

SLUICES
Gates built along drainage ditches to control the flow of water

DYKES
Drainage ditches

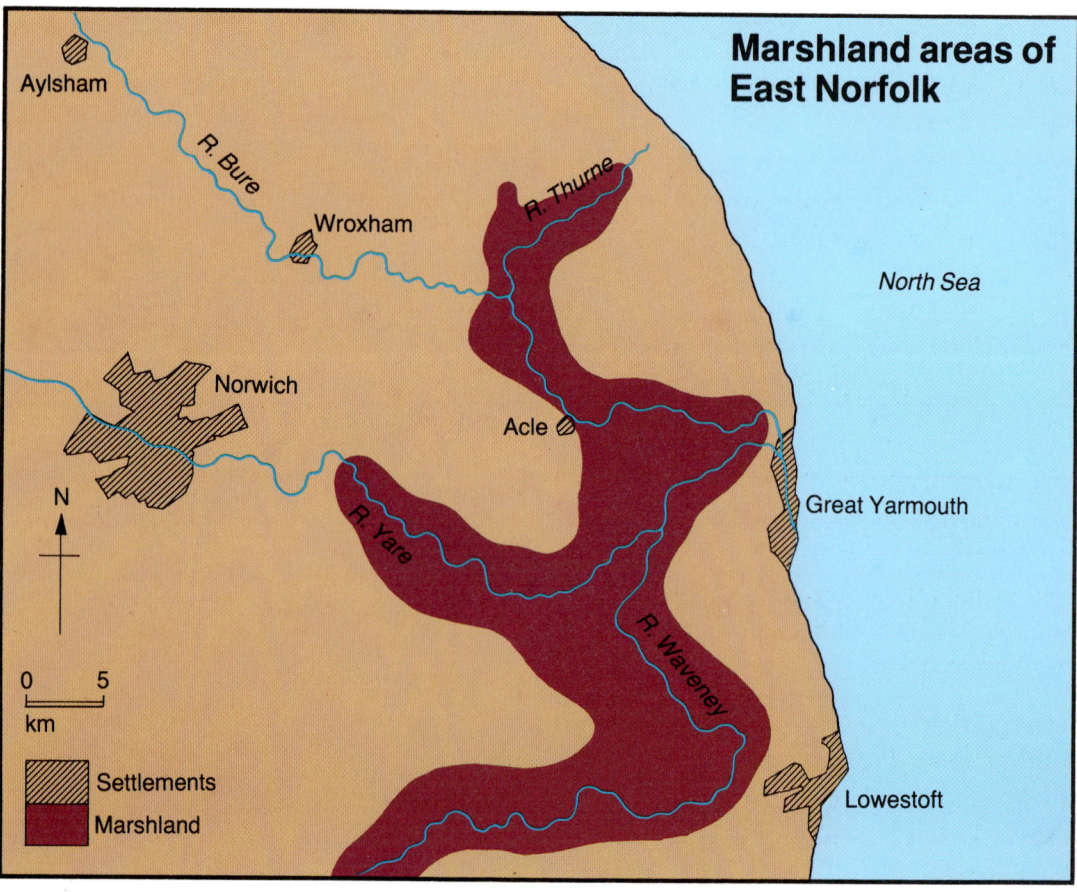
Marshland areas of East Norfolk

60

Halvergate Marshes, Norfolk

These areas are very attractive. Many people visit this area in order to view the wildlife. The marshlands are very important because of the variety of plant and animal life which lives in and around the drainage dykes. This is the HABITAT, or living area, for many species of plant and animal life which can no longer be found in other lowland areas. Many species which are found here have been lost from other lowland areas because of the amounts of pollution.

Here are some examples of the wildlife which inhabit this marshland area.

Summer months – a wide variety of nesting birds including: Mute swan, Shoveller, Oyster catcher, Lapwing and Yellow wagtail

Most nest in the sides of DYKES or on grassy banks

Winter months – feeding and nesting areas for: Geese, Swans, Mallards and Golden plover

Besides these there are many PREDATORS such as the barn owl, heron and kestrel which feed on the large numbers of small mammals living in these areas.

1 Use an atlas to describe where you would find the marshland environments of Norfolk.

2 Look at the map opposite. Name the three main rivers which flow through this area of Norfolk.

3 Look carefully at the picture of Halvergate Marshes. Write down anything you find attractive or unattractive about the landscape.

4 What are these marshland areas mainly used for?

5 What was used to drain the marshes in the 17th Century?

6 From the information on this double-page, write a paragraph to explain why these areas are so important.

HABITAT
The area where an animal lives and feeds

PREDATOR
An animal which lives from killing and eating other animals

The changing marshlands

Over the past ten years some of these marshland areas have been changing. Instead of being used by farmers for PASTURE land they have been changed into ARABLE land. The main reason for this is that many farmers have been given money from the EUROPEAN COMMUNITY to stop DAIRY and beef farming and to start to grow arable crops like wheat and barley.

This has meant that the landscape in the marshlands is now different. The water level is kept down by using diesel or electric pumps. The drainage ditches have been filled in and many hedges pulled out to make the fields larger. To supply the electric pumps with electricity, power lines have been built across the landscape. New farm buildings are often found, barns to store hay or SILOS to store grain. In places the hedges have been replaced by wire fences to keep fields with animals separate from fields of grain.

The drainage ditches which were so common in the marshland environment were very important in providing food for the wildlife. The diagram shows a food chain which is common in the marshlands. This is just one example of how a heron would find its food.

PASTURE
Land used for grazing animals

ARABLE
Land used for growing crops

EUROPEAN COMMUNITY
Twelve European countries which work together to try and improve trade

DAIRY
Producing milk

SILOS
Tall containers used to store grain

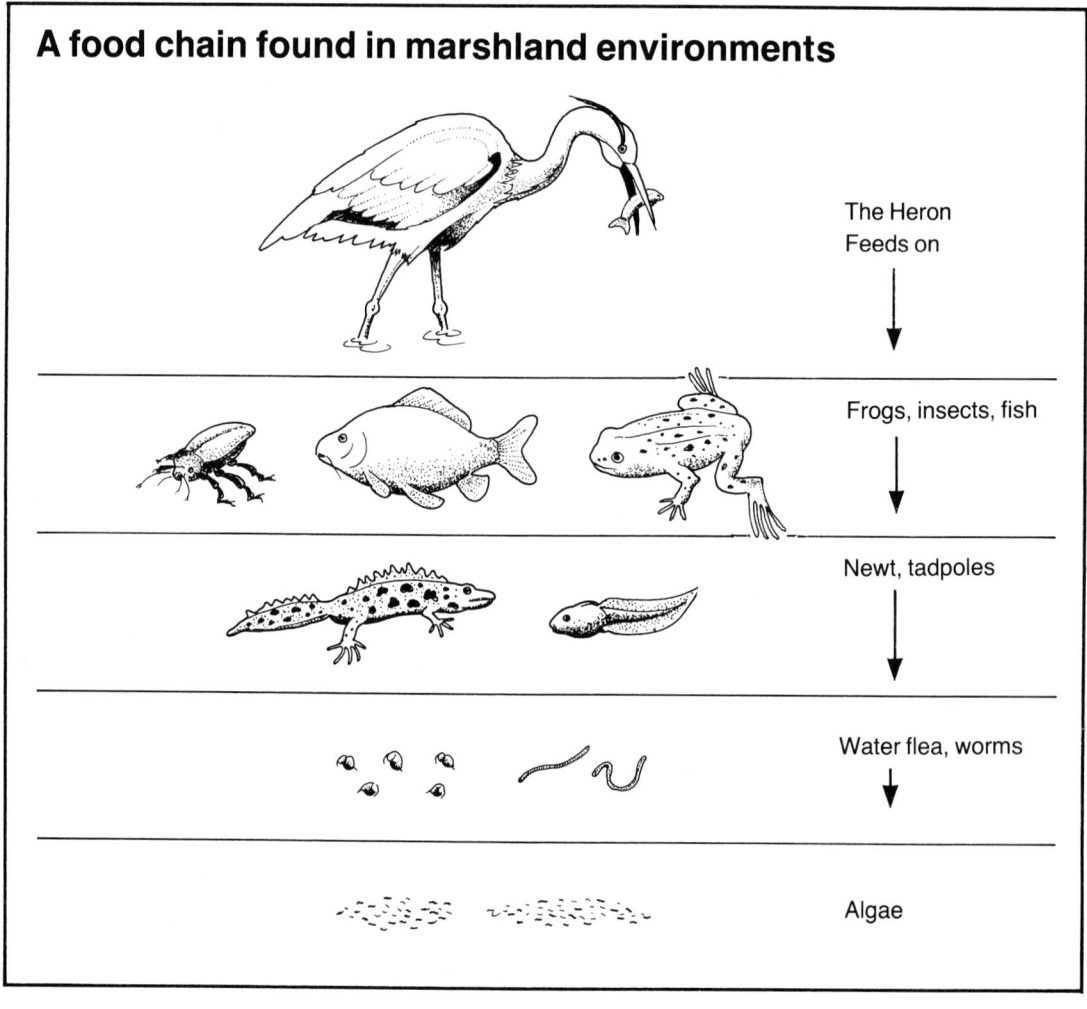

A food chain found in marshland environments

The Heron Feeds on ↓
Frogs, insects, fish ↓
Newt, tadpoles ↓
Water flea, worms ↓
Algae

1 How have the marshlands changed over the past ten years?

2 What is the main reason for that change?

3 How is the water level kept down when the marshlands are drained?

4 Look at the photograph of Halvergate Marshes on page 61. How will the landscape change?

5 By draining the marshes the natural habitat for a great deal of wildlife is spoiled. The diagram opposite shows a food chain which is often found in a marshland environment. Try and explain in your own words the meaning of the term 'food chain'.

6 Make a copy of the second cross-section in the sketch. Add labels to the arrows to describe any changes which have taken place.

7 Project idea: try and draw a food chain for another animal.

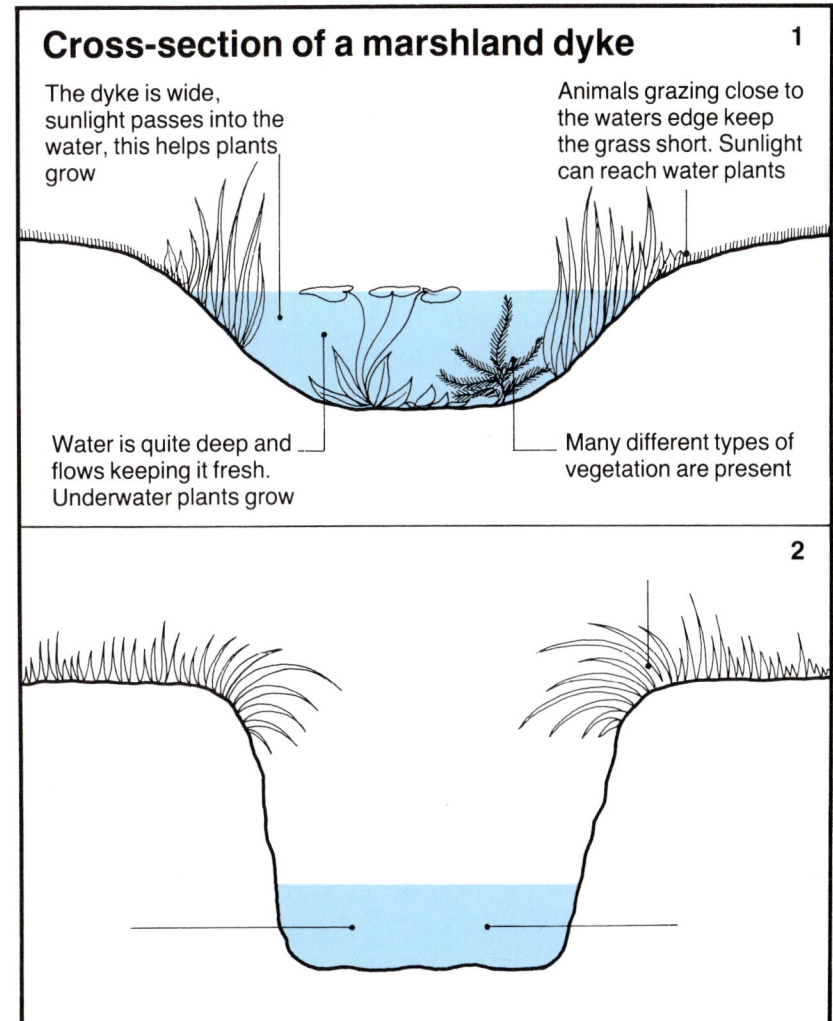

A Marsh Harrier

Investigating a landscape

A fieldsketch is a drawing of a landscape completed outdoors. The list opposite is a guide for you to follow if you ever draw such a sketch.

Equipment:

1 Sharp pencil
2 Rubber
3 Clipboard and paper.

Hints:

1 Draw the horizon first.
2 Add the largest features or lines which show a break in the view, e.g. buildings, hedges, dyke.
3 Complete the smaller detail, e.g. grazing cattle, clumps of grass.
4 The fieldsketch must be labelled clearly.
5 Give the sketch a title.
6 If possible show the direction, e.g. looking south.
7 Give a grid reference for the point from which the sketch was drawn.

A field sketch of a marshland environment by pupils at Castle Dyke School

When looking at a picture of a landscape it is possible to write down your feelings about that picture. A 'visual interest scale' is a table of different words which describe opposites, e.g. pleasant – unpleasant. Between the list of opposite words are five spaces. In the table here you could place a tick next to one of the five spaces which most describes your feelings towards the picture. (You can find another such table on page 24.)

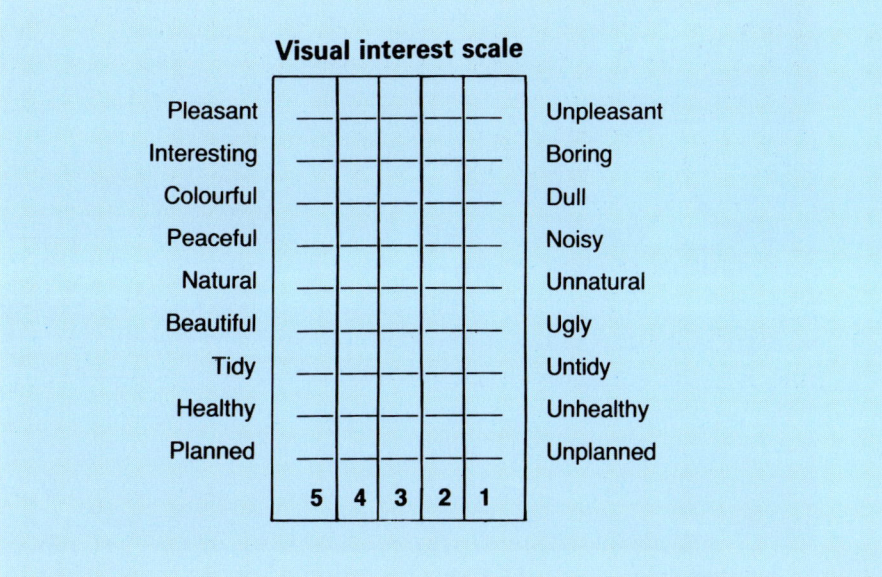

1 Using a full page in your book make your own copy of the fieldsketch – but this time with a difference! You should imagine that the landscape in the fieldsketch has been changed to an area of arable farming. Your sketch should have the following differences:

(a) No field boundaries.

(b) Fewer trees.

(c) Lower water level in the dyke.

(d) No grazing animals.

(e) Power lines and pumping stations.

(f) Grain silo and barn near to the farm buildings.

(g) Field planted with wheat.

(h) No birdlife.

(i) Tractor.

2 Using the photograph of Halvergate Marshes on page 61, carry out a visual interest scale and total your marks.

3 Do the same exercise for your sketch. Compare the results.

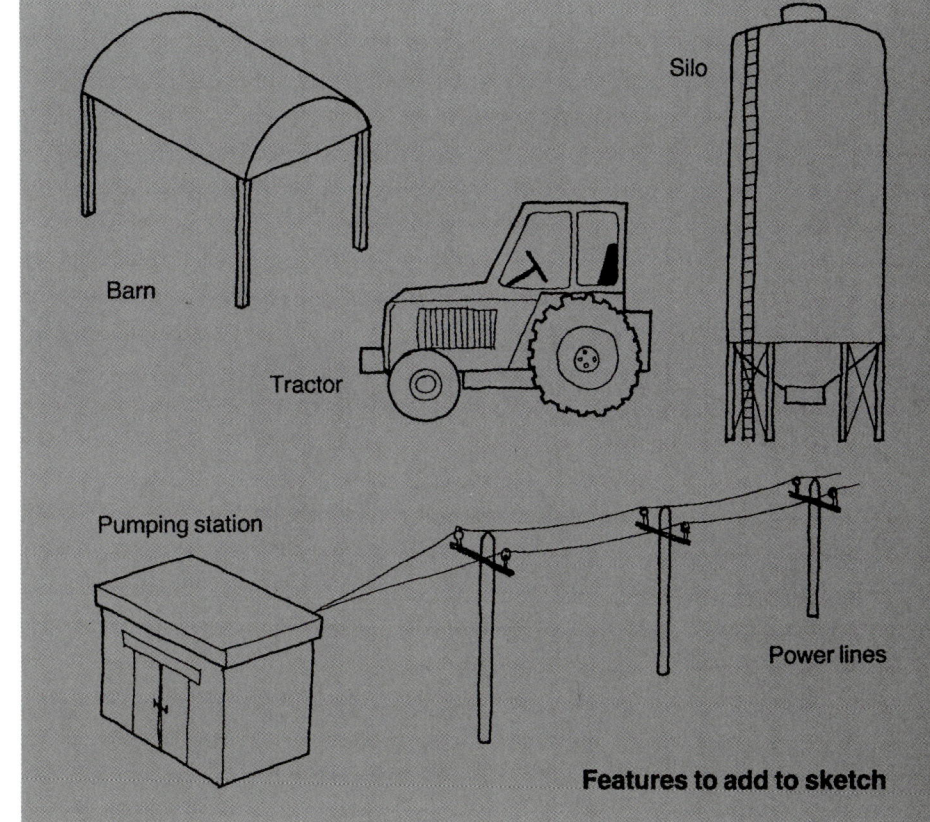

Features to add to sketch

65

An industrial estate

Edith Johnson has been an organiser for the local Ramblers' Association for many years. She is in her early sixties. Ms Johnson is a keen lover of wildlife and spends a great deal of time painting wildlife in watercolours. She is very strongly against any changes which would mean losing the natural life of the area.

In February 1987 the government said that it would like to make changes to the way land is used in countryside areas. Over the past few years Britain and other countries in the European Community have produced too much wheat! You have most likely heard of the European 'grain mountain' on news programmes. To reduce the amount of land being farmed the government are suggesting various possibilities: some of the farmland with poorer soils could be used for forests; some could be used for new housing or industry; and some could provide recreation land, e.g. golf courses.

Jean and Frank Newton own the farm in the lowlands which the Property Company wish to buy. The family own a number of farms in this area. They are very keen on keeping the farm and the landscape as it is. The Company have offered them quite a lot of money to sell a large part of one of their farms so they can build the industrial estate.

PROPERTY COMPANY
A company which buys land or buildings in order to build new houses, factories or offices

INDUSTRIAL ESTATE
An area of land where new roads and small factories are built

A large PROPERTY COMPANY from London want to build an INDUSTRIAL ESTATE close to a village in the Norfolk countryside. At the moment the land is being used for grazing cattle. The landscape is very similar to that shown in the fieldsketch drawn by pupils of Castle Dyke School. There are a number of people in favour of building the industrial estate and a number against. In order to discuss this problem thoroughly a public meeting is to be held at the local Town Hall. Here are some of the characters to be present at the meeting.

Jack Hardcastle is the local Member of Parliament. He has been the MP for this area for 14 years. The Government (his party) are very keen on encouraging businesses to build industrial estates in areas where farmland is poor. Mr Hardcastle soon hopes to get promotion and become a government minister. Many of the local people he represents are against any changes which would alter the character of the area.

Albert Ludham has worked for Jean and Frank Newton for many years. All his working life has been spent as a dairy farmer. His knowledge and skill in this type of work is very good. Mr Ludham loves this type of work. If the farm was sold he would lose his job. At the age of 54, with no other skills, he would find it difficult to get another job.

Marjorie Graham works for the Property Company which wants to buy Frank Newton's farm. She is in the area to discuss the possible sale with Mr and Mrs Newton and show details of her plans to the local council. Ms Graham has worked for this company for 7 years since leaving university. She is a good person at expressing her ideas. She will stress the good points of building the industrial estate and in particular the idea of creating new work in the area.

Either: Divide into groups of at least five.

(a) Five people choose each of the five characters shown in the pictures and read the information about that person.

(b) Many farms (not just the one on which Albert Ludham works) are threatened with change. A public meeting has been called at the local Town Hall to discuss the possible changes and for everyone to 'let off steam'. The following are the main characters.

J and F Newton – local farmers
A Ludham – representing local farm workers
M Graham – representing property company
E Johnson – representing the local ramblers
J Hardcastle – Chairperson and MP

Plan what each member of the meeting would say and use a tape recorder to record your ideas.

Or: Write a newspaper report describing the events of the public meeting.

Unit 8 UPLANDS

Using the uplands

Where to build a reservoir

An ideal area for a reservoir
- Underlying rocks which are IMPERMEABLE
- Heavy rainfall and many streams to keep the reservoir full
- Narrow steep-sided valleys which are easy to dam
- Valleys in highland areas to allow water to run downhill to lowland cities without pumping
- A cool area of the country so that less water is lost from the reservoir by EVAPORATION

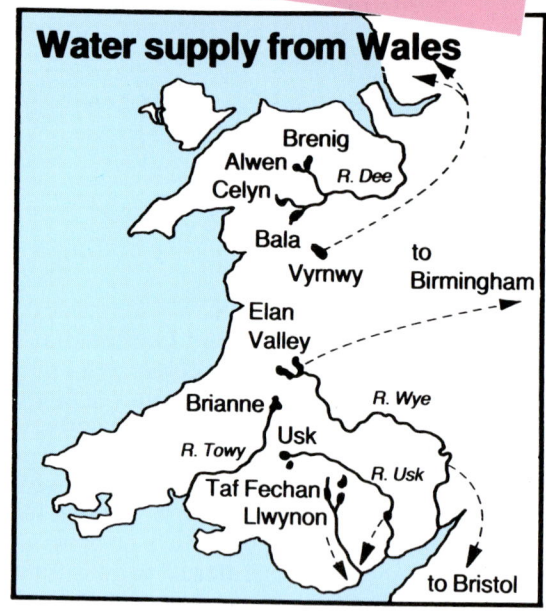

Water supply from Wales

As towns and cities grow, more water is needed for homes and industry. Much of our water is collected in reservoirs and it is piped to where it is needed.

Where should these reservoirs be built?

Lake Vyrnwy is built on impermeable rock like all reservoirs. It is one of the largest reservoirs in Wales.

1 (a) Look at the photograph of lake Vyrnwy and write down the first five words you think of.

(b) Join with a friend. Close this book. Now describe the photograph to your friend. How much of the photograph did you remember? Open the book and look at the photograph again.

2 Use an atlas to find the city that Lake Vyrnwy supplies water to.

3 (a) Study the photograph and map on this page and the information about rainfall on the map on page 40.

(b) Write out the five facts which make an ideal area for a reservoir.

(c) Tick those which are true for the area of Wales in which Lake Vyrnwy is situated.

IMPERMEABLE ROCK Rock which will not allow water to pass through it

EVAPORATION Heat causes water to turn to vapour and rise into the air

Lake Vyrnwy

Is the reservoir built in a valley with steep sides?

A narrow valley is easier to dam. A valley with steep sides will hold a large amount of water in a smaller area. There will be a smaller surface from which water can be evaporated. Also less land is lost.

4 We can find out if Lake Vyrnwy is in a narrow valley with steep sides. To do this we draw a cross-section from the map.
(a) Place the folded edge of a piece of paper along line A, B.

(b) Mark every place where a contour line meets the folded edge.

(c) Label the marks with the height of the contour as shown in the first diagram below.

(d) Draw a framework like the one in the second diagram. Transfer your marks and heights to the bottom of the frame.

(e) Draw faint vertical lines from each mark to the correct height on the frame and put a cross.

(f) Join up the crosses with a smooth curved line. On the drawing notice what happens when two crosses are on the same line.

(g) (i) Look at your cross-section. Lake Vyrnwy is in the valley. Is the valley narrow with steep sides?
(ii) Copy and complete this sentence. The Lake Vyrnwy valley is ___ with ___ sides.

(h) The depth of the reservoir is 25 metres. Show this on your cross-section by drawing the surface of the lake at the 250 metre contour and shading the area below the line.

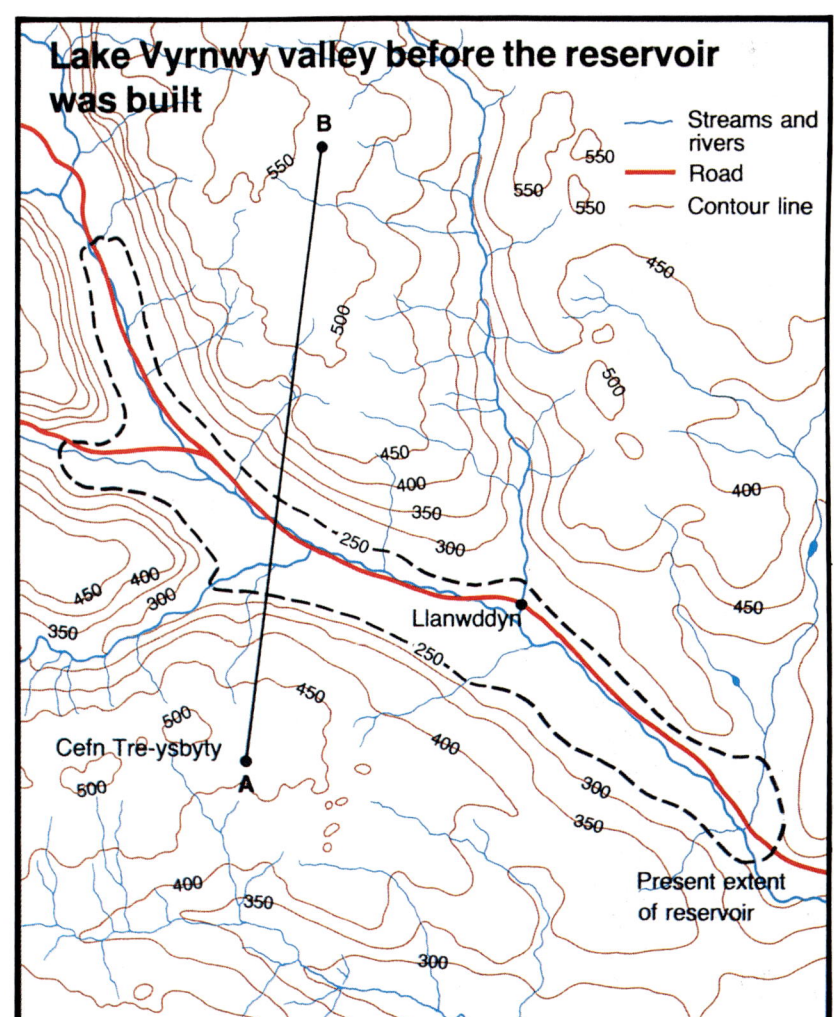

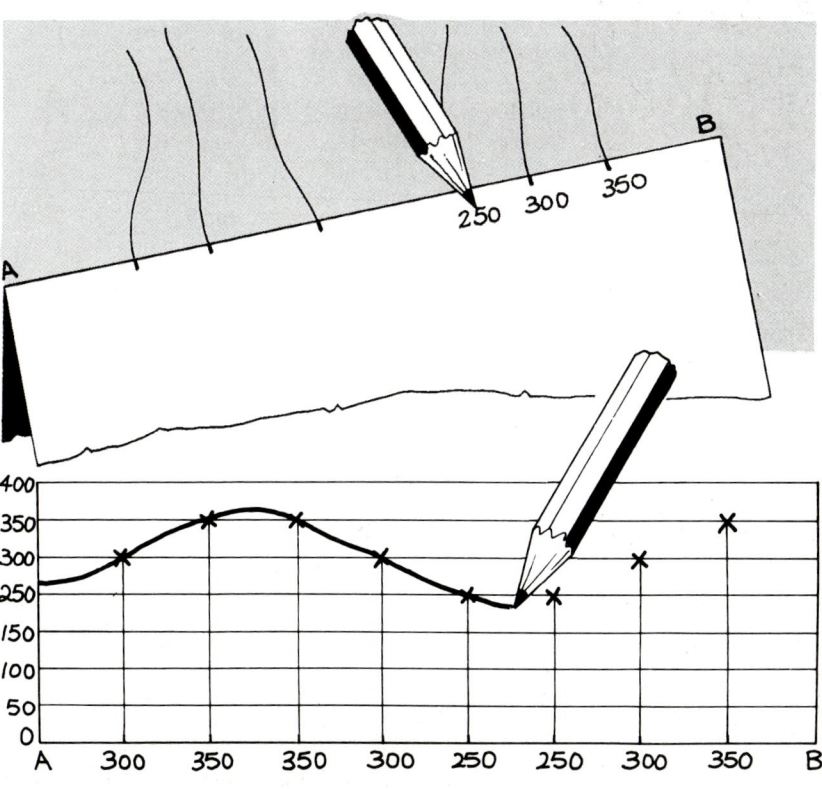

Glaciation

Snow collects in hollows on a mountainside. As it thaws water runs into cracks in the rock. The water then freezes and splits off pieces of rock making the hollow larger. As the snow builds up it becomes snow-ice called nevée. Snow-ice will move.

The snow-ice moves slowly out of the hollow and down the mountainsides as a glacier. As it goes it scrapes away at the side of the valley. Pieces of rock become trapped in the ice. They tear away at the valley sides.

The rock which is worn from the valley is called moraine. This is taken down the sides and underneath the glacier. The moraine is finally deposited at the bottom of the mountain. Here the temperature is higher and the ice melts.

A glaciated valley in Wales

AVALANCHE
A mass of snow which falls down a mountainside

MORAINE
Rock and debris which the glacier erodes from the mountain sides is deposited on the sides of the glacier as **Lateral** moraine or underneath the glacier as **Ground** moraine or carried in the ice to the end of the glacier and deposited as **Terminal** moraine

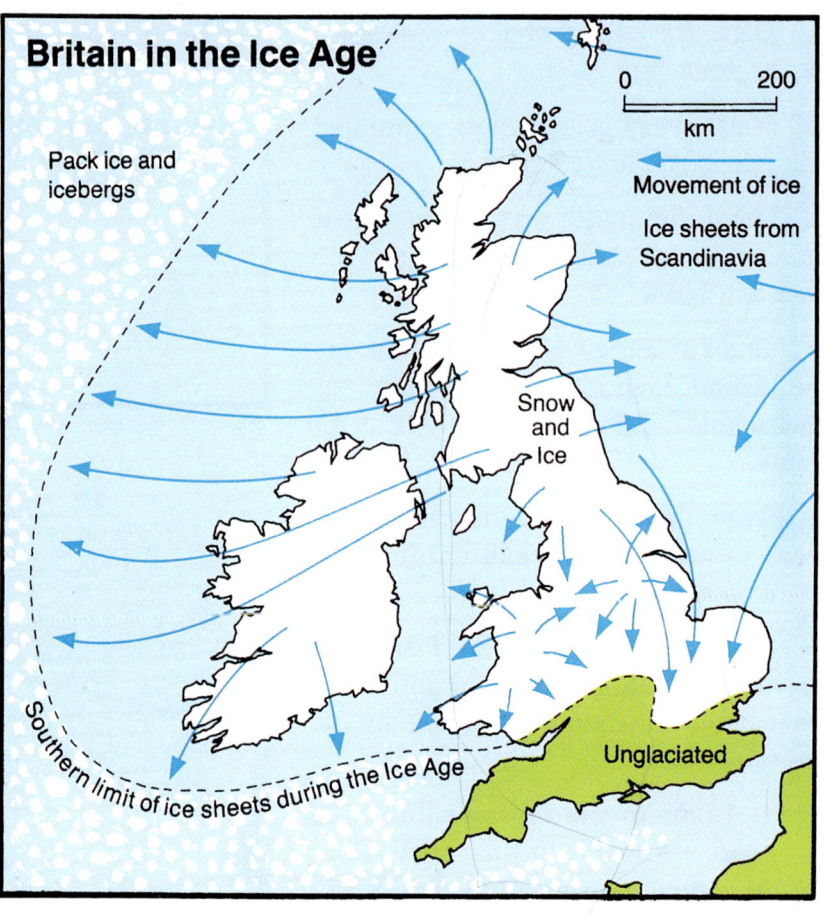

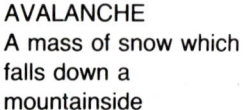

A cross-section of a glacier

How the narrow steep-sided valleys of North Wales were formed

Before glaciation

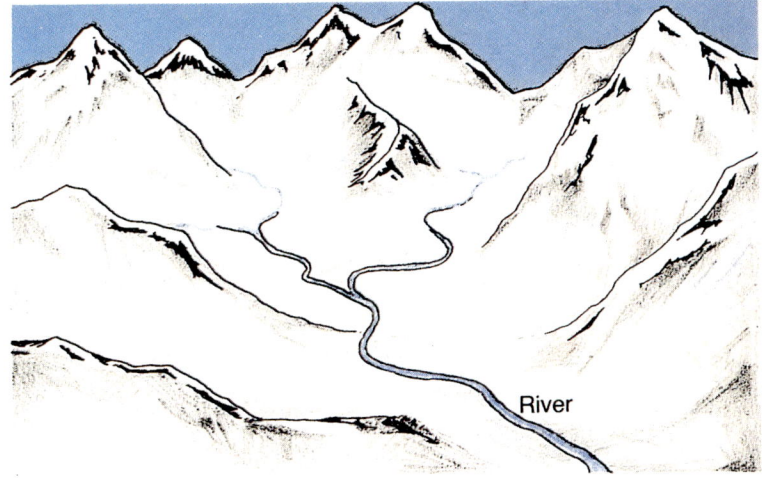

During glaciation

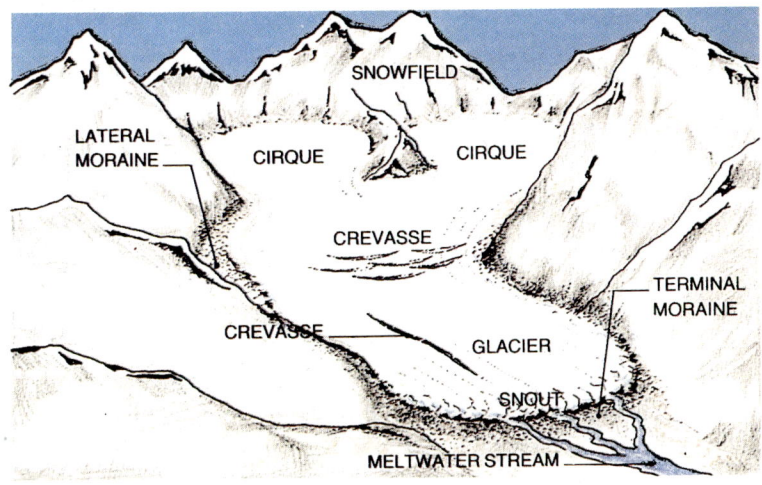

After glaciation

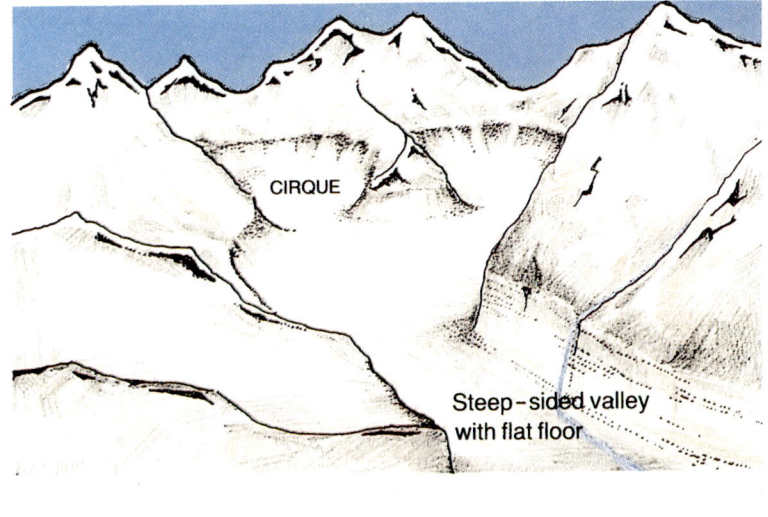

1 Look at an atlas and the map of Britain in the Ice Age.
(a) Write down the names of five towns in Britain which were **not** covered in ice.

(b) During the Ice Age was the place where you now live covered in ice?

2 (a) Copy the diagram 'A cross-section of a glacier' (p. 70).

(b) Label the features shown by the arrows. Use the diagram 'During glaciation' to help you.

3 Read the information on glaciation and pick out five words or phrases which you think best help to describe how glaciers change the shape of the land.

4 Join with a friend. Look at the landscapes in the diagrams 'Before glaciation' and 'After glaciation'. Make a list of the differences.

5 Draw a sketch of the photograph of a glaciated valley in Wales. Use the words below to label your sketch. Add other labels which you feel are important. Steep valley sides with little vegetation; Flat valley floor; Stream along valley floor.

SNOWFIELD
A large area of snow which never melts

CIRQUE
A large hollow formed by ice and frost at the start of the glacier. When the ice melts a large hollow or cirque with steep sides and a lake in the bottom is left behind

CREVASSE
A large deep crack in the surface of a glacier

SNOUT
The lower end of the glacier

MELTWATER STREAM
A stream of water at the end of the glacier which flows from the ice as it melts with the rise in temperature as the glacier reaches lower levels down the mountainside

A site for a reservoir

Join with three other people to form a group of four. Firstly work in pairs. One pair investigate the suitability of Llangynog for the proposed reservoir. The other pair investigate the suitability of Aber-Cywarch for the proposed reservoir (see page 74).

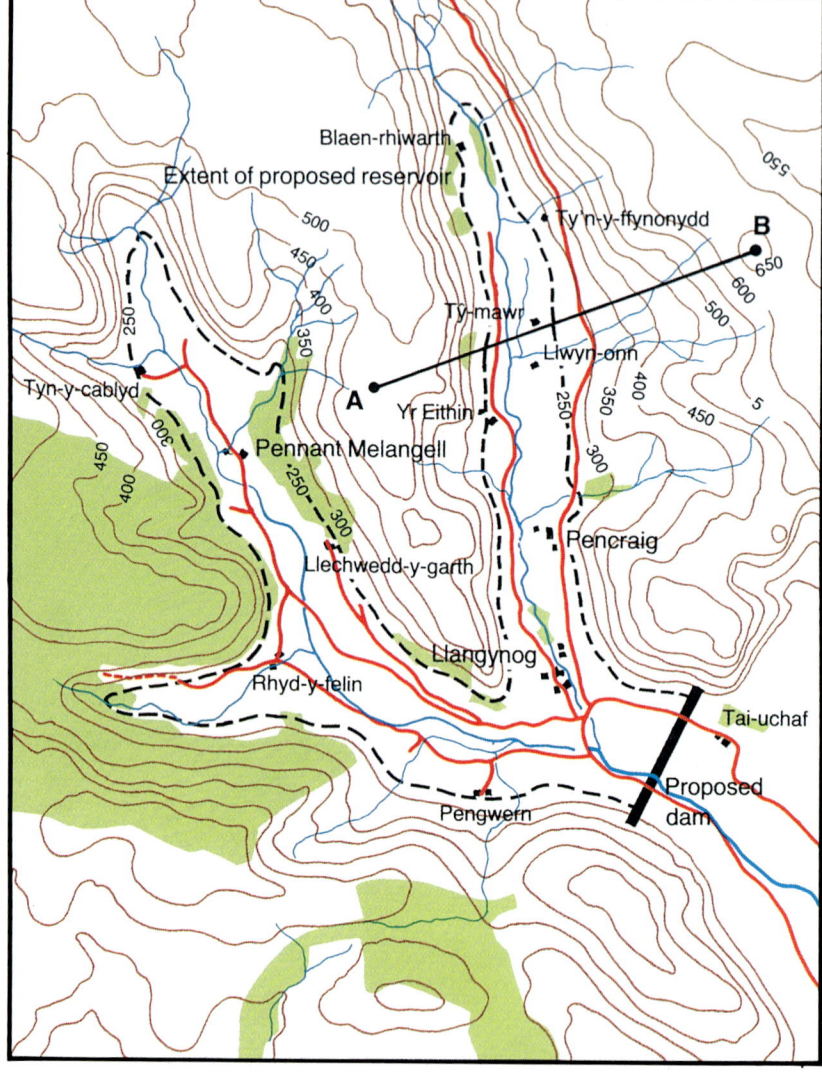

Llangynog

1 Draw a cross-section from A to B on the map.

2 Look at your drawing of the cross-section. Do you think this is a glaciated valley? Give two reasons for your answer.

3 Fill in the table below from the information given on the map.

Number of streams bringing water to the reservoir	
Number of farms lost	
Number of villages lost	
Number of roads needing to be re-routed	

4 Make a table like the one below. Read the information on the opposite page and fill in the columns 'For' and 'Against' building in this valley.

FOR	AGAINST

Now turn to page 74

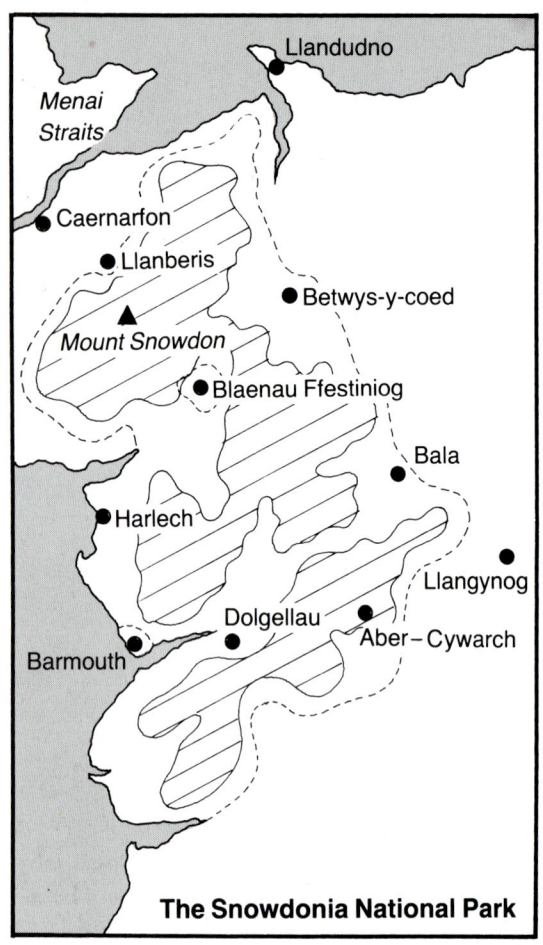

The Snowdonia National Park

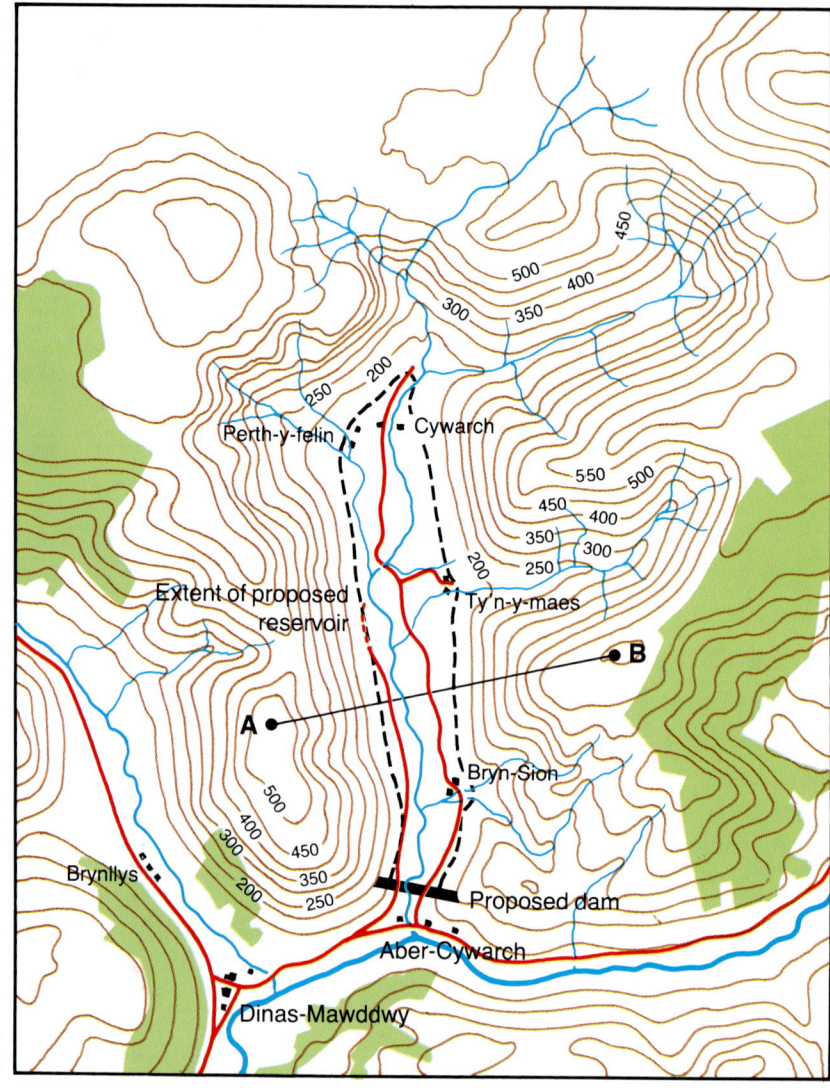

Aber-Cywarch

1 Draw a cross-section from A to B on the map.

2 Look at your drawing of the cross-section. Do you think this is a glaciated valley? Give two reasons for your answer.

3 Fill in the table below. Use the information given on the map.

Number of streams bringing water to the reservoir	
Number of farms lost	
Number of villages lost	
Number of roads needing to be re-routed	

4 Make a chart like the one below. Read the information on the opposite page and fill in the columns 'For' and 'Against' building in this valley.

FOR	AGAINST

Now turn to page 72

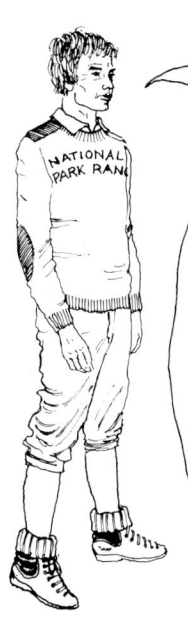

NORTH WALES GAZETTE, 24 JULY 1987

RESERVOIR SCHEME

NOW A CHOICE BETWEEN TWO VALLEYS

A reservoir is to be built here in North Wales. The choice lies between two valleys. In one valley the village of Llangynog. The other valley lies in the Snowdonia National Park.

We have been looking at the two sites and have done our own survey. This shows that if the Llangynog site is chosen the homes of over 300 people will disappear under the water of the lake. If the Aber-Cywarch site is chosen only 75 people will lose their homes.

Both valleys are in beautiful countryside. Our survey shows that four times as many visitors enjoy the Aber-Cywarch valley than the Llangynog site. A National Park officer says "Large numbers of walkers and climbers come to the Aber-Cywarch valley. The only road will be drowned if the reservoir is built."

We counted the traffic on the roads through the valleys. Our results are shown in the table below. There is no doubt that if the Llangynog site is chosen a new road will have to be built. If it is not there will be a long detour for the traffic.

Some people question whether a reservoir is needed at all. Once it is built another Welsh valley will be lost forever.

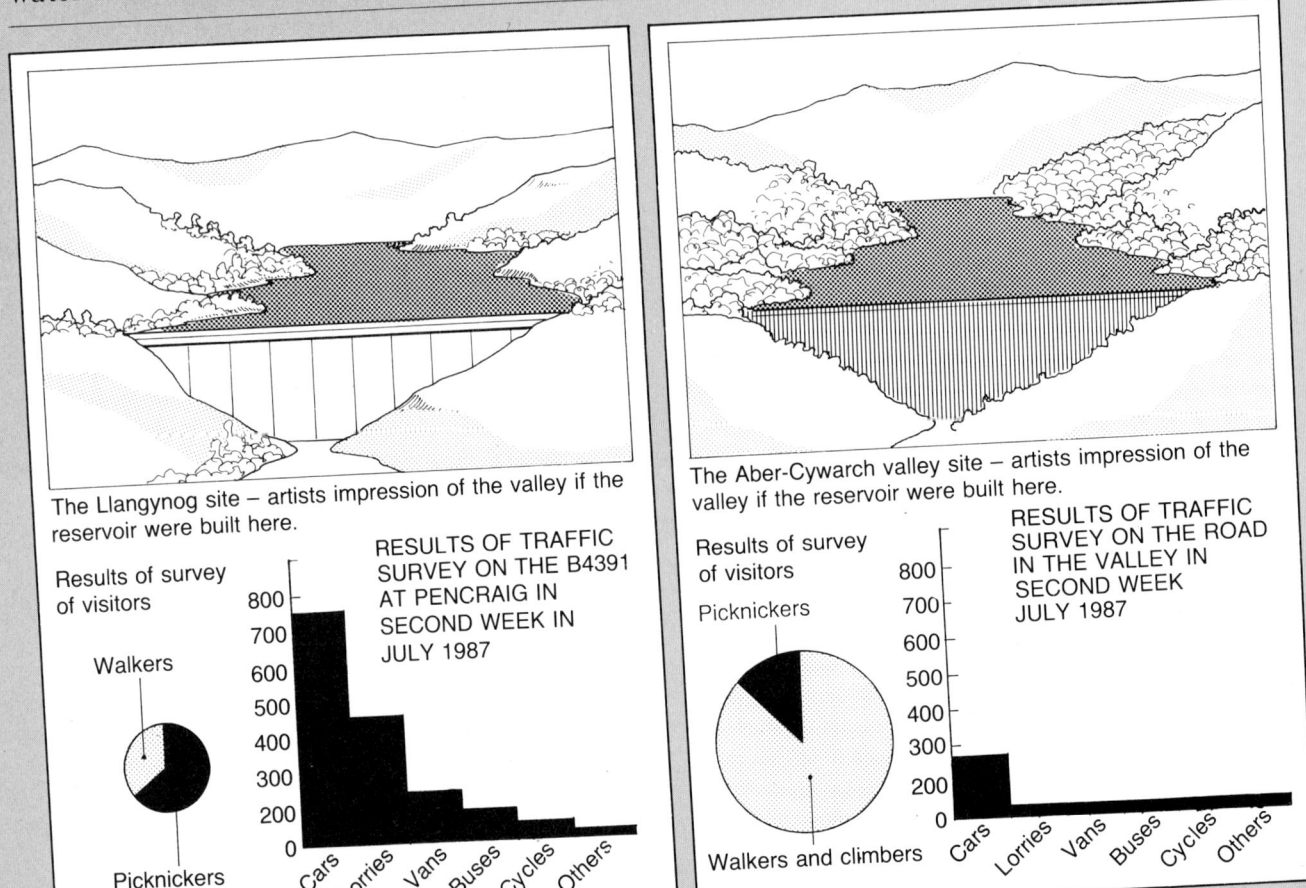

The Llangynog site – artists impression of the valley if the reservoir were built here.

The Aber-Cywarch valley site – artists impression of the valley if the reservoir were built here.

Results of survey of visitors

RESULTS OF TRAFFIC SURVEY ON THE B4391 AT PENCRAIG IN SECOND WEEK IN JULY 1987

RESULTS OF TRAFFIC SURVEY ON THE ROAD IN THE VALLEY IN SECOND WEEK JULY 1987

The size of the circle shows how many visitors come to the two valleys.

Which site?

1 Go back to your group of four. Each pair of the group of four should now show the evidence they have collected to the other pair in your group.

2 Together read the newspaper story on the opposite page. Use the article to add to your evidence about how suitable each site is for the reservoir.

3 Work in your group of four.

(a) Draw out the table on this page.

(b) Read the comments in the table.

(c) For each comment give a score out of five for each site. Give a high score for a comment if you think the site is a good site from that point of view.

(d) Add up your scores.

(e) Look at your scores and the other evidence you have collected. Decide which of the valleys is the most suitable place for the reservoir.

4 Be ready to explain to other groups your reasons for choosing this site.

Comment	Llangynog Points	Aber-Cywarch Points
Narrow, steep-sided valley		
Good rainfall		
Many streams bringing water to the reservoir		
Many farms will be drowned		
A village will be drowned		
The rocks are impermeable		
The reservoir will drown the best farm land		
Many people will loose their jobs		
A main road will need to be diverted		
The valley is beautiful scenery which should be preserved		
The valley is inside the National Park		
Total		

Decision – the best site is?

Unit 9

LANDSCAPES

Two contrasting areas

A group of students from Manor School investigated the differences in the two areas on the maps. They studied: **Soil**, GEOLOGY, **Water**, **How people use the land**, **Vegetation**, **Landscape**.

They took photographs of the two landscapes and labelled the main features.

Landscapes can be different even if they are close to each other and at almost the same height. Such landscapes can look different and be used in different ways.

1 Join with a friend to find differences between the two areas shown on these maps. To help you:
(a) Draw a table like the one below.

(b) Count how many of each feature there is on each map. Write the numbers on the table.

(c) Write three sentences about the differences between the two map areas.

2 Suggest labels for (a) (b) and (c) on the photographs opposite.

3 Look at the two photographs. Make a list of the differences between the landscapes.

4 In order to obtain a feeling for the landscape and its quality the students worked out an environment survey. First they made a visual interest table like the one below using pairs of opposite words to describe the landscape. You could add extra words if you wish.

Feature	Map A	Map B
Stream		
Village		
A class road		
Other roads		
Reservoir		
Dale		
Edge		
Farms		

	Scores							
	3	2	1	0	1	2	3	
Interesting								Boring
Attractive								Ugly
Quiet								Noisy
Welcoming								Hostile
Clean								Filthy
Rugged								Smooth
Untouched								Spoilt
Like								Dislike
Safe								Dangerous
Spectacular								Ordinary
Varied								Monotonous
Unpolluted								Polluted

GEOLOGY
The rocks which make up the Earth

The students then looked at each photograph. Between each pair of words they placed a tick. The tick shows how the word describes the landscape: 3 very well, 2 quite well, 1 is not very well, and 0 if both words describe the landscape

(a) Complete the table for each photograph using different coloured ticks for each. Compare your results with a neighbour.

(b) Use the table to write a paragraph about your feelings for the landscape and its quality.

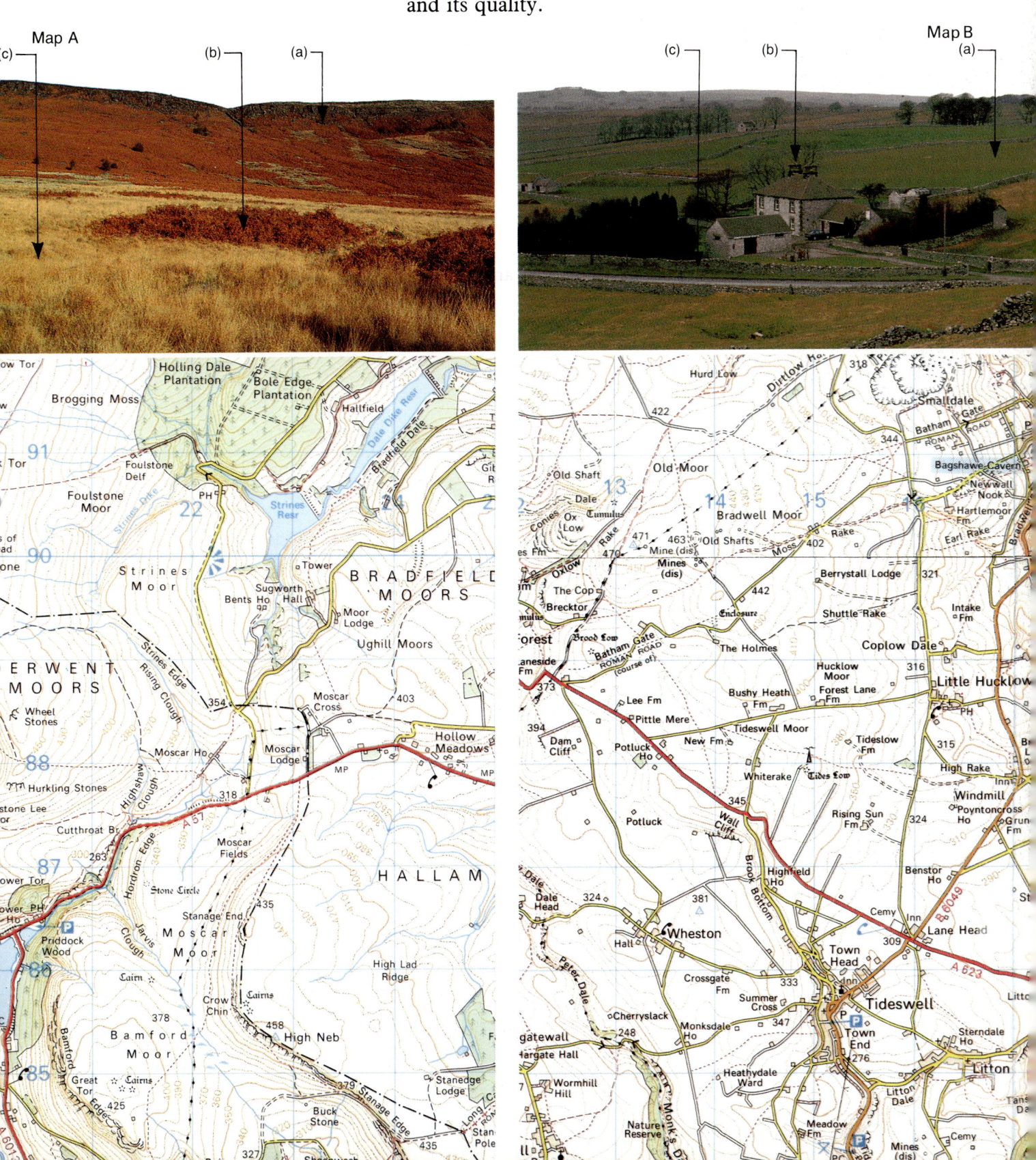

The rocks beneath our feet

Area A

The students studied the rocks in the two areas. In Area A they found a rock known as millstone grit.

1 (a) Copy the 'Rock sample investigation chart'.

(b) Complete the sections on 'Colour' and the 'Hand lens magnified description'.

2 Use the information on the chart to describe millstone grit.

3 Look at the labels on the diagram of 'The formation of millstone grit'. Write out the labels in the correct order, 1 to 4, to show how millstone grit was formed.

4 How does the photograph help show how millstone grit got its name?

Millstone grit

Gritstone

Rock Sample Investigation Chart

Touch – Rock felt rough and gritty

Colour –

Hardness – Copper coin will not scratch the gritstone

Hand lens magnified description –

Test with dilute hydrochloric acid – No reaction

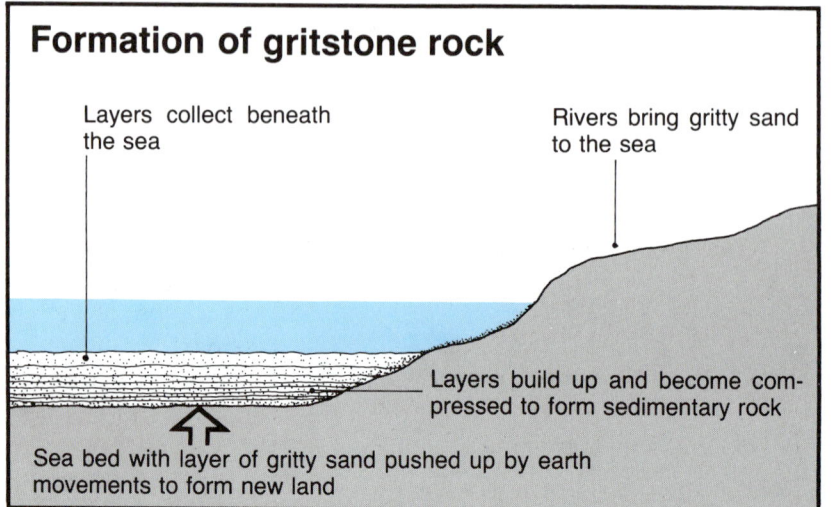

Formation of gritstone rock

- Layers collect beneath the sea
- Rivers bring gritty sand to the sea
- Layers build up and become compressed to form sedimentary rock
- Sea bed with layer of gritty sand pushed up by earth movements to form new land

Making landscapes

Gritstone

The students of Manor School looked at the gritstone. They could clearly see two outstanding landscape features.
1 They noticed many streams flowing in small valleys over the gritstone.
2 At the end of the gritstone there were steep edges.

Two of the photographs they took are shown here.
With them is an explanation of what the students found.

1 Look at Map A on page 79. Count the number of streams you can see on the map.

2 Name the edges you can see on the map.

3 Using the photograph of an edge describe what an edge is like.

A gritstone edge

Layers of sedimentary rock were pushed above sea level. They were then folded or bent upwards. This formed the Pennine Hills. The highest parts of this upfold were worn away. This left the limestone in the centre and the gritstone on the sides. Where the gritstone was worn away edges were formed.

A valley on gritstone rock

Rain-water runs over the land or through the soil. It collects in small streams. They flow over the gritstone which is an IMPERMEABLE ROCK. The streams carry very small pieces of rock with them. Sometimes when there is a flood and the stream has more energy quite large rocks are rolled along. These rocks wear away at the bed and sides of the stream. As this happens the sides of the valley collapse and the stream wears a deeper valley in the rock.

Area B

In Area B the students found a rock known as limestone in which they found many fossils.

5 On a copy of the 'Rock sample investigation chart', complete the sections on 'Colour' and the 'Hand lens magnified description'.

6 Use the information on the chart to describe limestone.

7 The sentences describing the formation of limestone rock are in the wrong order. Re-write them in the correct order.

8 (a) Which of the fossils shown on this page is a coral?

(b) Which fossil is found in the rock sample shown on this page?

9 Draw a labelled sketch of the photograph.

A limestone quarry

Limestone

Rock Sample Investigation Chart

Touch – Rough and bumpy

Colour –

Hardness – Can be easily scratched by copper coin

Hand lens magnified description –

Test with dilute hydrochloric acid – Reaction with the chemical (a fizzing), the rock is dissolved by weak acid

Formation of limestone rock

Layers of sea creatures and corals become pressed together into rock.
Shelly sea creatures live in warm clear seas.
Layers of rock are pushed up to form new land.
Shells of sea creatures and corals collect at the bottom of the sea in layers several hundred metres thick.
Millions of shells of sea creatures collect on the bed of the sea.

Limestone fossils

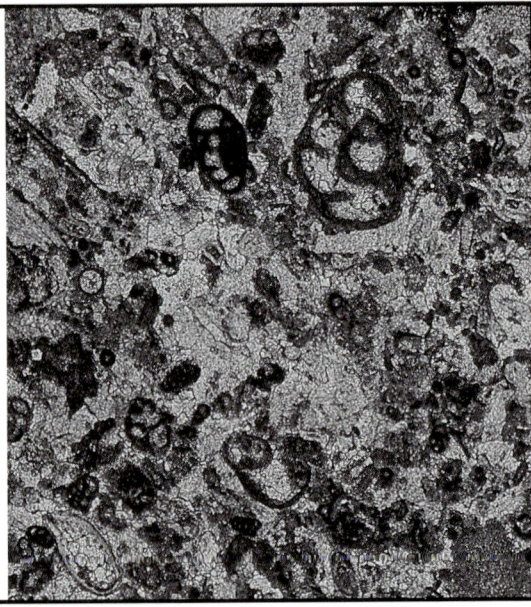

Crinoid

Brachiopod

Lamellich

81

Limestone

Next the Manor School students looked at the limestone features. They found that they had to go underground. This is what they found.

4 Draw a sketch of the photograph of the cave. Label the features it shows. Include labels which explain how the features were formed.

5 Compare the photographs of valleys in gritstone and limestone. Make a list of the differences between them.

6 Explain how a stalagmite is formed.

IMPERMEABLE ROCK
Rock which will not allow water to pass through

PERMEABLE ROCK
Rock which allows water to pass through it

Caves, stalactites and stalagmites

Rain-water is a very weak acid. It flows through the cracks in the limestone. A little of the calcium carbonate in the rock is dissolved by the acid. This widens the cracks. Whole streams may flow underground forming large caverns. Water drips from the ceiling of the cave. A little of the calcium carbonate is left behind. This builds up until a stalactite is formed. When a stalactite and stalagmite join a pillar results.

Limestone is a PERMEABLE rock. Rain-water moves along the cracks in the rocks gradually widening them. Many rivers and streams flow underground. During the ice age there was so much water on the land that the cracks were full. The streams flowed over land and formed valleys which are now left dry.

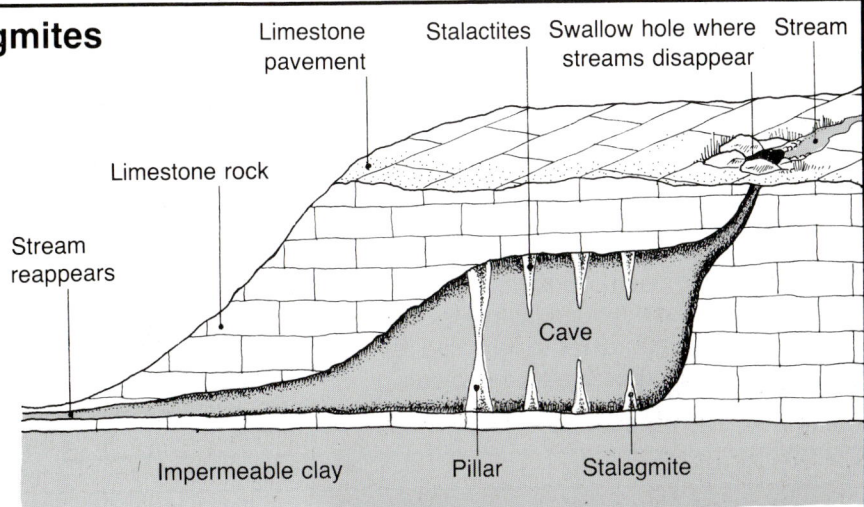

Cave (right) with stalactites and stalagmites

A dry valley in limestone (below)

Vegetation and soils

RANDOM
Points chosen completely by chance

The Manor School students investigated the vegetation and soils in the two survey areas. They carried out two experiments at different levels on a slope in each area.

Experiment 1 – vegetation
To find which are the main plants growing in an area.

A quadrat is used. This is a one metre square frame. It is divided into a grid with strings 20cm apart. The quadrat is placed on the ground at RANDOM points. A long knitting needle is dropped from each place where the strings cross. The plant the needle touches is recorded. In this way a sample of the type of plants growing is collected.

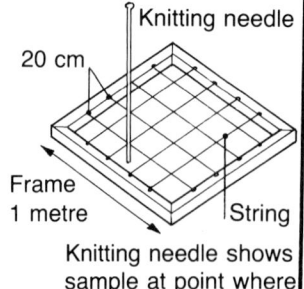

Knitting needle shows sample at point where strings cross

Experiment 2 – soil
To find the type of soil in the area. (Permission is needed before doing this experiment.)

A pit is dug down to the underlying rock. The depth of the A and B layers in the soil is then recorded.
A The humus layer – the surface
B The layer with pieces of rock and little humus
C The underlying rock

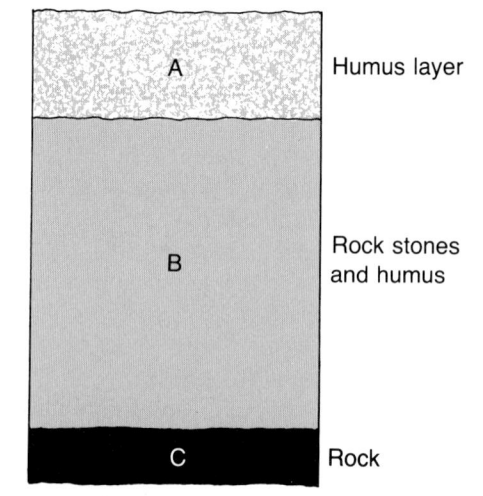

Gritstone area A

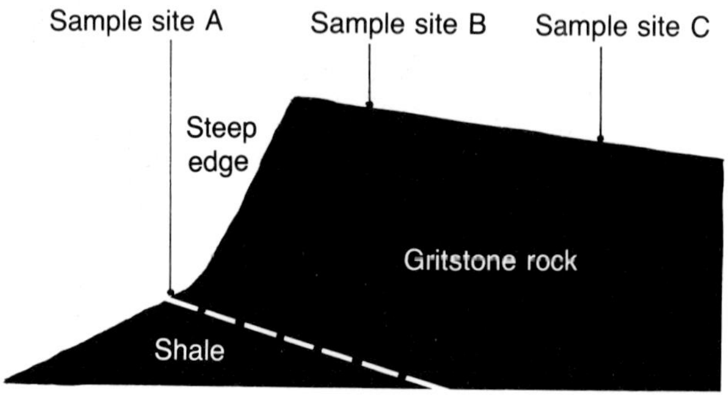

Sample site A, Sample site B, Sample site C — Steep edge, Gritstone rock, Shale

Soil type — Sample site A, Sample site B, Sample site C
Scale: 1mm represents 2cm

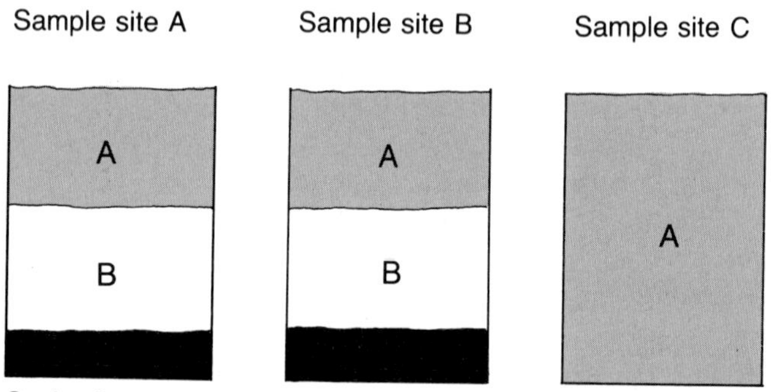

Key: Heather, Bracken, Bilberry

Vegetation type

Sample site A — Survey 1, Survey 2, Survey 3
Sample site B — Survey 1, Survey 2, Survey 3
Sample site C — Survey 1, Survey 2, Survey 3

No of each species (0–40)

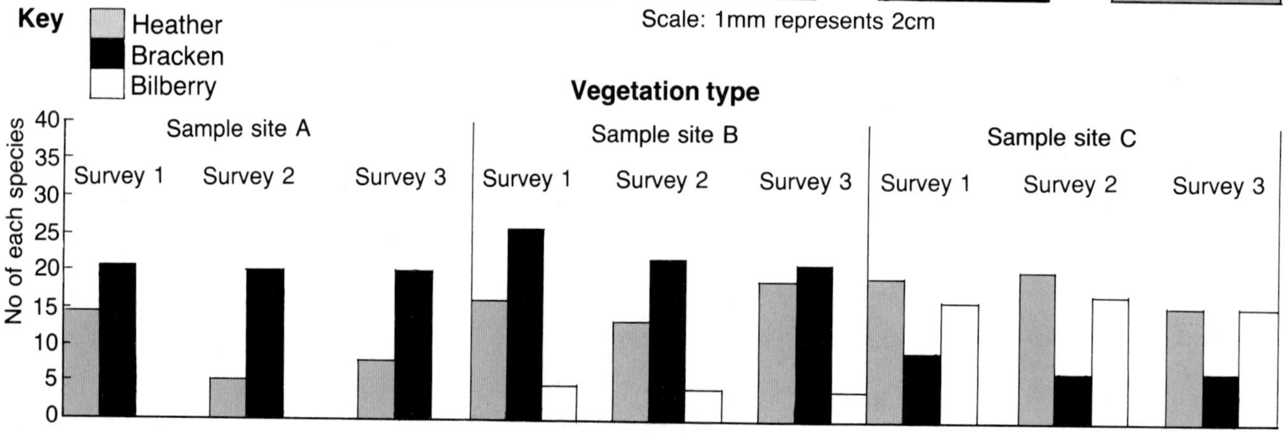

1 Look at the results the students of Manor School obtained on the gritstone.
(a) How does the vegetation change from point A to C?
(b) How does the soil change from point A to C?

2 (a) Plot the information gained from the limestone quadrat survey on a graph like that for gritstone.
(b) Does the vegetation change from points A – C on your graph?

3 Look at the types of vegetation found on gritstone and limestone.
(a) Make a list of the differences in vegetation.
(b) Now make a list of similar types of vegetation.

4 (a) Draw a soil profile diagram for limestone soil at sample site A and site C. Use the information given on this page.
(b) What differences do you notice in the soils on gritstone and those on the limestone?

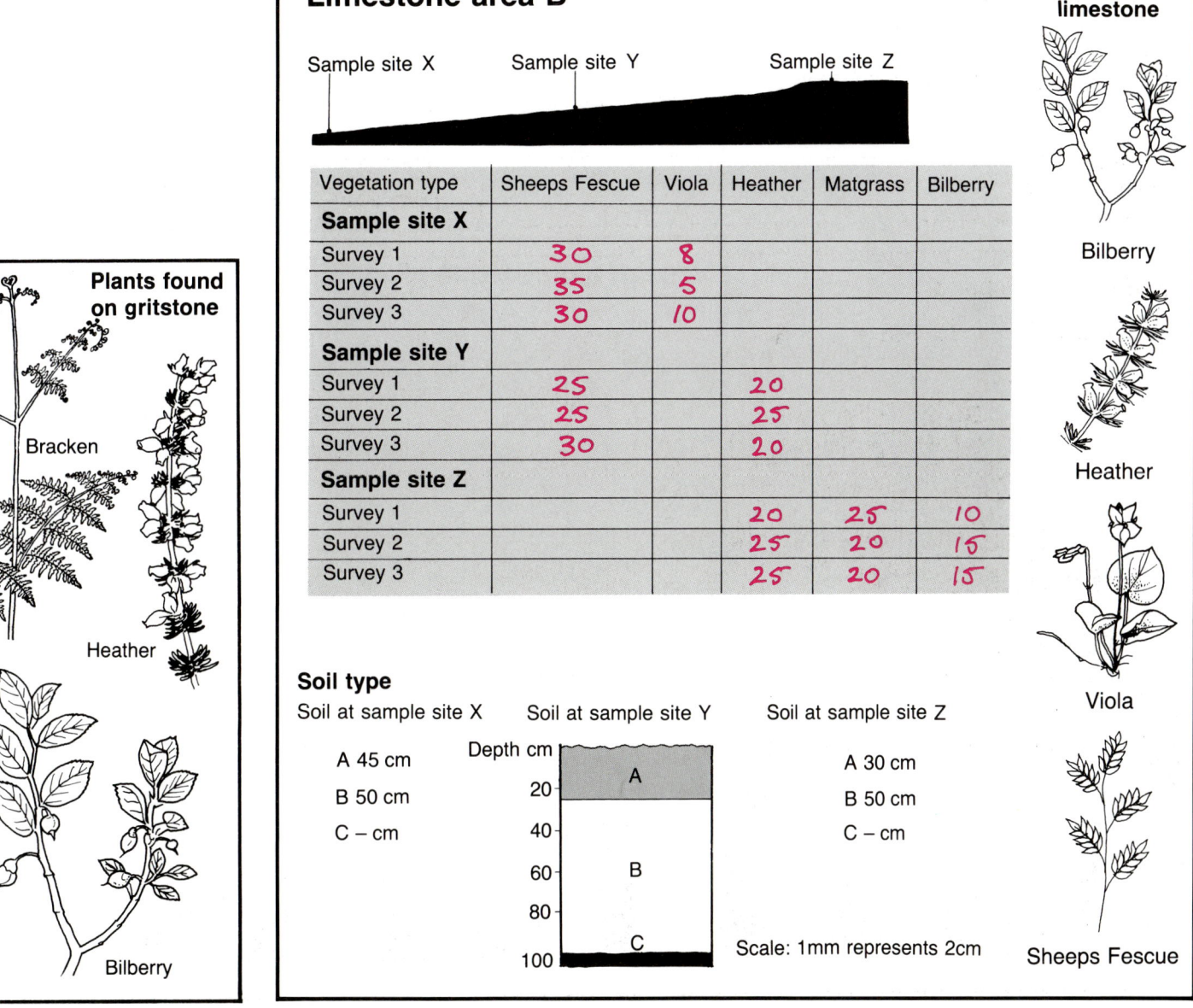

Limestone area B

Plants found on limestone

Sample site X   Sample site Y   Sample site Z

Vegetation type	Sheeps Fescue	Viola	Heather	Matgrass	Bilberry
Sample site X					
Survey 1	30	8			
Survey 2	35	5			
Survey 3	30	10			
Sample site Y					
Survey 1	25		20		
Survey 2	25		25		
Survey 3	30		20		
Sample site Z					
Survey 1			20	25	10
Survey 2			25	20	15
Survey 3			25	20	15

Soil type

Soil at sample site X
A 45 cm
B 50 cm
C – cm

Soil at sample site Y
Depth cm
20 — A
40
60 — B
80
100 — C

Soil at sample site Z
A 30 cm
B 50 cm
C – cm

Scale: 1mm represents 2cm

Plants found on gritstone: Bracken, Heather, Bilberry

Plants found on limestone: Bilberry, Heather, Viola, Sheeps Fescue

Using landscapes

We can see patterns on the landscape. They are often a result of how people have used that area. Walls are built by farmers for instance.

The students of Manor School saw all the activities shown in the sketch when they were studying the gritstone area.

1 List all the ways in which people are using the gritstone landscape.

2 Which of the activities you have listed change or leave a mark on the landscape?

3 (a) Copy the sketch of the limestone landscape. When the students from Manor School went there they saw people using the area.
(b) Draw the people on the limestone landscape to show the possible activities taking place there.
You could change the drawing if you wish.

4 Which part of the landscape is most changed by the activities of people? Give reasons for your answer.

5 Join with a friend. Look at the two diagrams. On the diagrams eight sites are shown by the letters A to H. Copy the list of features below. Next to each feature put the letter A to H. Choose the letter from the diagrams which shows the best site for that feature.

Climbing, Picnic site, Caving, Hang gliding, Car park, Reservoir, Dairy farming, Visitors centre

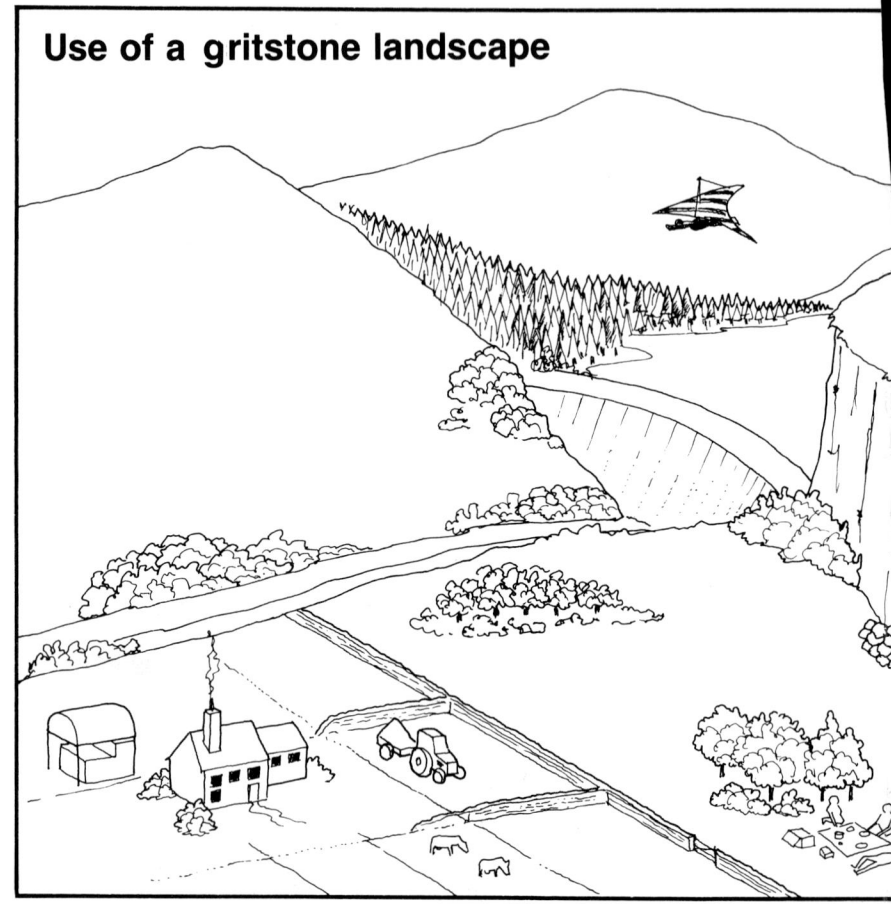

Use of a gritstone landscape

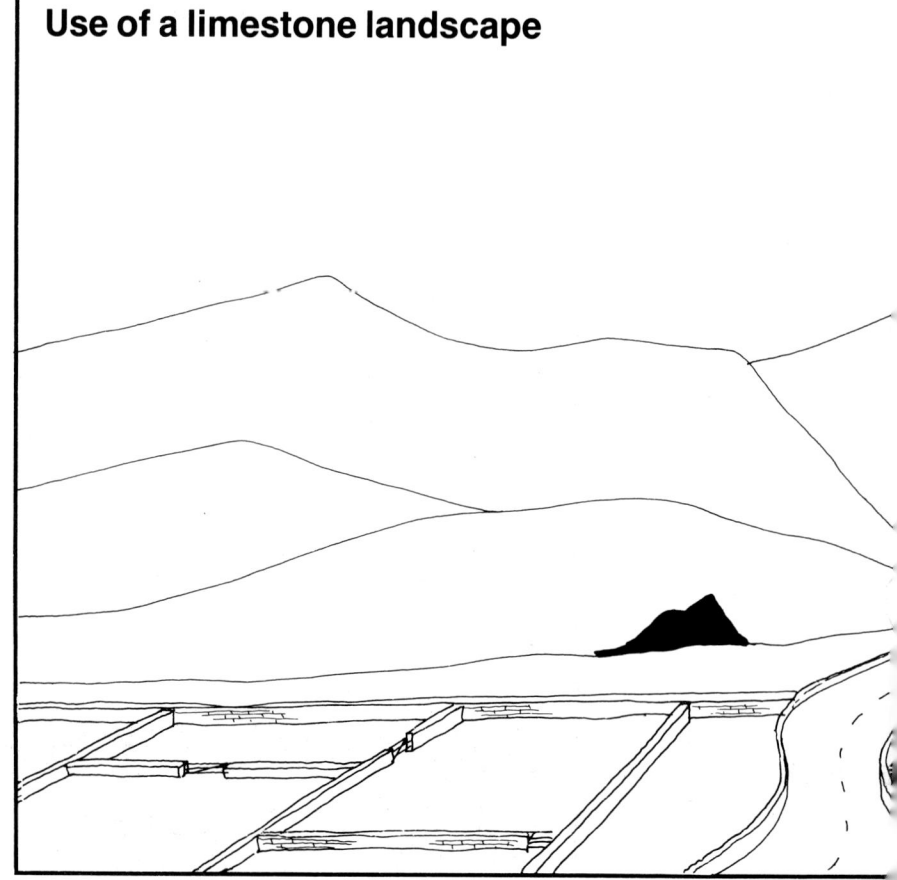

Use of a limestone landscape

Diagram of gritstone area

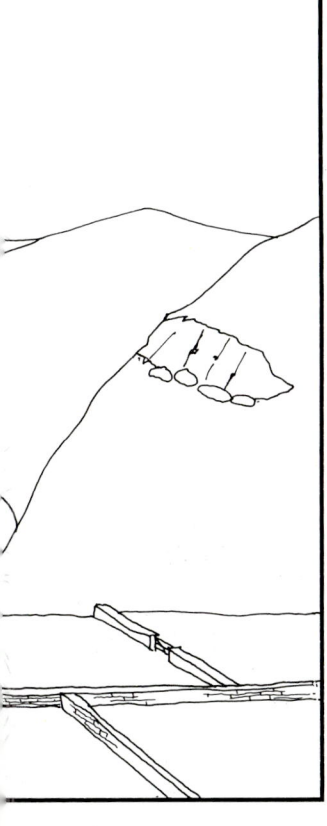

Diagram of limestone area